how to
sell
your
CRAFTS ONLINE

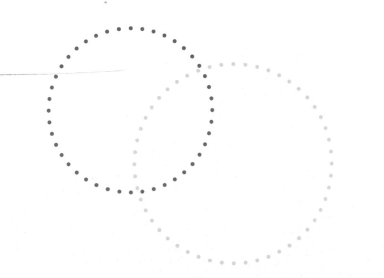

A Step-by-Step

Guide to

Successful Sales

on Etsy

and Beyond

how to

SELL

your

CRAFTS ONLINE

Derrick Sutton

St. Martin's Griffin

New York

Design by Susan Walsh

ISBN 978-0-312-54126-2

First Edition: October 2011

10   9   8   7   6

To Lora, Mum, Dad,
Maja, Inez, Jeni,
Queen Badger, and Auntie Gaye
(for your eagle eyes!).
I also dedicate this with heartfelt
thanks to Andrea Hurst, for
inspiring writers on
the pier, and to
everyone at Just
Write!

Acknowledgments

I WOULD like to thank my wife, Lora, my Aunt Gaye, my agent Andrea Hurst, BJ Berti and Jasmine Faustino at St. Martin's Press, as well as everyone who generously agreed to be included in this book.

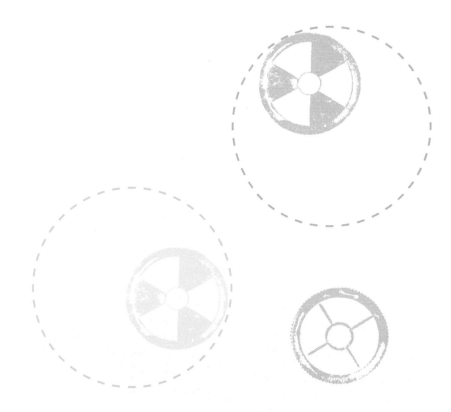

Contents

Author's Note

THE PURPOSE of this guide is to illustrate techniques for the initial online setup for an Etsy shop and promotion of handmade items online.

Etsy is a site that is based in the United States but used internationally by both buyers and sellers. Because of the seemingly endless possible creations and locations from all over the world, there are many issues that a seller might encounter that are far beyond the scope of this book.

It is very important that you research and fully understand your local, state, and federal laws in regard to issues like (but not limited to) proper business practices, business license requirements, tax codes/collection, zoning, permits, liability insurance, postal regulations, product safety, and materials laws such as the Consumer Product Safety Improvement Act or California's Prop 65, as well as all user agreements and the terms and conditions of any Web sites or services that you decide to sign up for.

Information that you post online will be available and visible to the public at large, so if you choose to do so please use good common sense and discretion.

This book has been written from my personal observations of selling and promoting an Etsy shop. Neither myself, the techniques I share, or this book have been endorsed or are in any way affiliated with Etsy.com.

Please note that some of the Web sites and screenshots you will see in this guide may have changed since the time of writing. Given the ever-changing nature of the Internet, this is outside of my control. The URLs and Etsy shop names used in this book are fictitious at the time of printing and have been made up strictly as an example teaching tool. If you have any questions, then please feel free to contact me at the Web site which I have created to support this book:

http://howtosellyourcraftsonline.com/

how to
sell
your
CRAFTS ONLINE

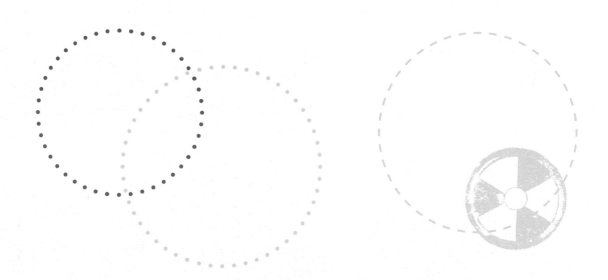

Introduction

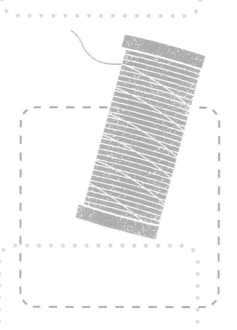

SELLING your art, crafts, and designs has never been easier. There are now huge opportunities for creative people to not only sell their work to a staggering range of highly targeted buyers but also to use the Internet to build a loyal and attentive online following. In the not-too-distant past your options were limited to craft fairs or local shops, word of mouth, or stores willing to sell your items (often for a hefty commission).

Today, the Internet has opened up a great window of opportunity for creative sellers and you now have a chance to showcase your talent before thousands of eager consumers.

You can set up your own Web site for a very affordable sum of money, but if you don't have the time, money, or inclination there are a number of online venues that are fully dedicated to artists and crafters, which will help sell your items for a reasonable fee.

Initially eBay became a site where artists and crafters could sell their work, but because eBay is primarily geared towards auctions it was not always an ideal venue to sell handmade items.

Everything changed in 2005 with the advent

of Etsy, a marketplace dedicated to buying and selling all things handmade. The site has seen a meteoric rise and shows no signs of slowing. People are attracted to buying on Etsy for many reasons and certainly the ease with which you can buy both unique and affordable items is a strong factor, but so, too, is the sense of community within Etsy.

Etsy has a rather unique proposition, since there are not many other retail outlets where you get to make such a personal connection and communicate directly with artists who are also sellers. Etsy's thriving community of artists and enthusiasts of all things handmade can become both addictive and highly rewarding.

You may wish to sell your art or crafts for a variety of reasons. Perhaps you create for fun and your house is being overrun with your works of art (a houseful of sock monkeys can be a problem!) or maybe you're an artist or photographer and you want to build an online presence and reach a wider audience. Your creative business may be a supplement to your income, or perhaps it's a full-time job.

Whatever your niche, craft, or creative expression, online marketing is vital to expanding your audience. In this book you will learn:

- The quickest and simplest way to optimize your Etsy shop for online exposure
- How to generate traffic and bring potential buyers to your Etsy shop
- Quick and straightforward ways to stand out from your competition
- The best way to photograph your items and key mistakes to avoid
- How to get the most from your listings using highly effective copywriting secrets
- How to gain an instant snapshot of your shop and where you need to focus your efforts
- Why blogging can give your Etsy shop a boost in traffic and sales
- How to place your Etsy shop on the map for local shoppers
- A strategy for securing your own Web address, which hosting site to use, and how to set up a blog with a one-click install
- Easy ways to create a wealth of fresh and relevant content and never suffer writer's block!
- Tips to improve your blog and help it to rank high within the search engines
- How to find the best "Web 2.0" sites and how they can direct a high amount of targeted traffic to your shop
- The effective way to use Facebook and Twitter and why so many people get it wrong
- How to make a video showcasing your creativity and upload it to YouTube
- How to write articles about the subjects you love, have them published, and increase your visitors and potential customers

If you're new to Etsy, you can follow the advice given in each of the chapters and ensure your shop is fully optimized by the end of each lesson. If you already have an Etsy shop or are an experienced seller, then I still suggest you take the time to follow along with each of the techniques in this book. While some of the suggestions may seem obvious, the devil is in the details and sometimes the simple techniques are overlooked.

No matter how little experience you have using the Internet, this book has been written and designed to teach practical lessons with a low learning curve. These are techniques that can be put into practice as you read through the chapters and they will start working immediately. One of the best things about working on the Internet is that you have an amazing sense of leverage. As you send a "tweet" or share content on your Facebook Page, the work is amplified by as many people as you're connected to. The key is to connect with as many people as possible, and I will show you how.

The best way to work through this book is one chapter at a time. There will be no chance of overwhelm or information overload if you take each step slowly. Read through, implement the lesson, and move on.

By the time you've finished reading this book you'll have a strong grasp of online promotion and will have learned many practical techniques, which will help people find your unique handmade items.

You've put your blood, sweat, and tears into your work, so you deserve to find the largest possible audience to share your creativity with!

So let's turn to chapter 1, where we will consider the best name for your Etsy shop—a name that will summarize your creativity and build your online brand.

Naming Your Etsy Shop

1

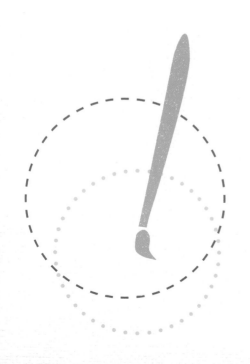

IF YOU haven't yet set up a shop on Etsy, you will need to visit the link below and fill in the details. One of these steps will be choosing a shop name, so I recommend you read this chapter before completing this step.

www.etsy.com/register.php

If you already own an Etsy shop and are experiencing low sales, then you may wish to open a new shop using the techniques in this chapter.

Name

When it comes to choosing a name for your Etsy shop and for your Web site (which will be covered in more detail in a future chapter), it's really important that you take some time to find the best option: one that will both represent the items you're selling as well as help you rank in the search engines.

Take time to make a list of your most common items; is there a theme or "keyword" that can act as a neat summary for your creations?

Sometimes you may find Etsy shops whose shop names have very little in common with the products they are selling, and in terms of a shop being optimized for the Internet this can be counterproductive.

When it comes to choosing a name for your Etsy shop, you can use a keyword, which may help you to rank in the search engines. Or perhaps you prefer something more fun or personal, e.g., using your own name for your shop. Let's look at both options.

KEYWORD

A keyword, in terms of the Internet, is a word that the search engines use to categorize and decide what a Web site, or piece of content or article, is about.

If, for instance, you're selling photographic art prints, then your keywords would be "Photographic Art"; if you were selling handmade Celtic jewelry, then your keywords would be "Celtic Jewelry." This may sound obvious, but working out the essence of what you're selling and choosing keywords will help you with the topics throughout this book, as well as give you a boost when it comes to placement with the search engines.

You could use your keywords within the title of your shop; for example, if you were selling fine art, you could call your shop something along the lines of "Fine Art by———", or if you were selling handmade tote bags, you could call the shop "Tote bags by———."

This may sound unimaginative, but it can tell visitors to your shop, in a glance, exactly what you're selling as well as helping the search engines decide where your shop fits within their rankings.

The sample Etsy shop I'm going to use throughout this book is selling sea glass jewelry. So if I chose the shop name "Sea Glass Jewelry Box," I would be using my keywords "Sea Glass Jewelry." The search engines would "read" the shop title and this would give my shop a slight boost if I wanted to rank for the phrase "Sea Glass Jewelry."

Here's how my shop name would appear:

www.etsy.com/shop/seaglassjewelryboxexample

SOMETHING MORE FUN OR PERSONAL

However, you may wish to have a more thoughtful or imaginative name for your shop or perhaps, as mentioned, you want to build your brand using your name. This is fine, because the techniques and exercises in this book are going to help you optimize your shop for the items you're selling. Think of using your keyword in your shop title as a small boost in search engine optimization, rather than an essential decision.

The one thing to bear in mind is that you

should choose a brief, memorable name, which is both positive and appealing to your customers. You will also need to ensure that your shop name is between four and twenty characters long to fit within Etsy's requirements and bear in mind that, once you choose your shop name, it can't be changed at a later date.

A fun way to tackle this exercise is to brainstorm and write down a few names and options, perhaps using keywords as well as more personal choices, and then ask friends or family to help you decide.

A VARIETY OF ITEMS

But what if you're selling more than one item? You may be creating and selling both jewelry and artwork, so how do you choose a name for your Etsy shop? If you're an existing seller, then you could run a simple analysis of your shop and decide which item sells the most and is of the most interest to browsers and customers, as well as having the highest value. If you're new to selling, then you could still use the above solution, analyzing your items to see which of them you will be concentrating your efforts on and are going to be the most profitable.

If you're planning on selling more than one type of product and they have nothing in common, for example, sea glass jewelry and landscape photography, then there is no reason why you can't open two Etsy shops. The only thing you need to bear in mind is that you must link your shops by disclosing them in each shop's announcement.

If you're selling different items, then you can work towards your shop having a "theme," which will unite your creations. This can be achieved in a number of ways (all of which are covered in future chapters). A few ways to ensure your shop stands out from other sellers and has a strong sense of unity is your choice of shop name, distinct and sharp photography as well as the color schemes you use for backgrounds in your photographs, how you title your items, and your Etsy banner. If you tie all of these together, then your shop will have a distinctive and identifiable look and feel, even if you are selling different items.

If you take a little time to look at a cross section of Etsy shops, you will see how organized and well-presented some of them are, as opposed to the less well-planned shops, which can sometimes look fairly chaotic and haphazard and do not have a clear theme.

Whether you're going to start a new Etsy shop with a keyword-specific name or stick with an existing shop, you'll need to ensure your store is fully optimized for the search engines. This topic is covered in chapter 2.

A C T I O N S T E P S

- Find keywords that summarize your items for your Etsy shop name, or choose a warm, memorable, and professional name.

- Analyze a cross section of Etsy shops to see how other sellers represent themselves through their shop names.

- Get a second opinion—conduct a poll with friends, family, or colleagues and ask them to choose the best name for your shop from a list of brainstormed suggestions.

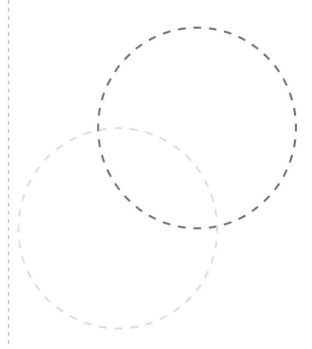

Search Engine Optimization

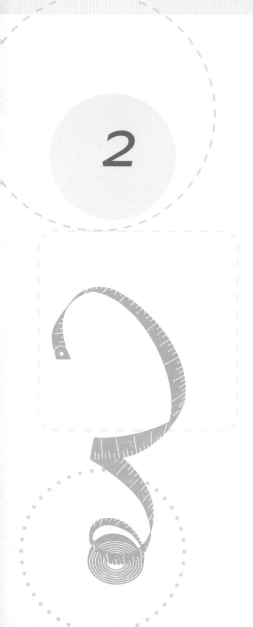

2

NOW THAT you've found a name for your Etsy shop, it's time to ensure maximum exposure in the search engines by optimizing your shop. Search Engine Optimization (or SEO) can sound a little daunting if you're new to the subject, but it's really very simple. It's like holding up a sign that tells the search engines what your Web site is about so that they can decide where to place you within their results.

There are several areas where you can place keywords within your shop that will optimize your shop and improve your ranking. The first one is your "title tag."

When you open a Web browser and visit a Web site, you can see its title tag in the top left-hand corner of your screen.

For example, visit Etsy's front page and look at the top of the screen and you should see the words "Etsy—your place to buy and sell all things handmade, vintage, and supplies." That is Etsy's title tag.

Title Tags

Your Etsy shop will have its own title tag, and ensuring that you're using a relevant keyword can help optimize your shop for the search engines.

To enter your title tag, you need to sign in to "Your Etsy," look to the left of the menu and under "Shop Settings," and click on "Info & Appearance":

On the next page, the first option under "Shop Info" is "Shop Title," and as you can see below I've entered my keywords:

Shop Title

Sea Glass Jewelry Box

If I had a shop name, I would write something like "Sea Glass Jewelry by———." Once you click on "Save" and click on your Etsy shop's home page (the page your customer sees), you should see your keyword in the top left-hand corner of your Internet browser.

The next place you need to optimize for your keyword is your shop announcement.

To set this up, click on "Your Etsy," look to the left, and under "Shop Settings" click on "Info & Appearance."

I've used my keywords in my sample shop announcement shown below. This is a really important field because it's the first thing people see; so you will want to spend some time and thought on the information you add. Not only do the search engines read this area, but so will potential customers, and while you need to include your keywords, you should focus equal attention on writing something that will captivate human readers.

In my example, I've used my keywords upfront by starting my announcement with them: "Sea Glass Jewelry."

Shop Announcement

Sea Glass Jewelry has been a passion of mine for as long as I can remember. I find these precious jewels of the sea fascinating and they have become my inspiration for the unique handmade treasures that I offer in my shop!

It's a good idea to keep your shop announcement brief. Occasionally I visit Etsy shops that have a huge block of text, and this can be a little overwhelming and off-putting, plus it pushes the listings farther down the page, where they may not be immediately visible.

Sections

The search engines also scan your shop sections, as shown in the following illustration:

Sections in this shop

« Shop home (all items)

Sea Glass Jewelry (0)

Sea Glass Earrings (0)

Sea Glass Pendants (0)

Sea Glass Necklace (0)

Sea Glass Ring (0)

Sea Glass Bracelet (0)

Again, I've ensured the words "Sea Glass Jewelry" are included in my first section because these are my main keywords. You will want to do the same, by including your main keywords in the first section and then creating related sections that utilize your other keywords.

For ideas for relating keywords, you could use the above example or get a wealth of relating keywords through Google Insights:

www.google.com/insights/search/

By adding your main phrase in the Google Insights search box, you can find related phrases.

To add new sections to your Etsy shop, log in, go to "Your Etsy," "Shop Settings," and "Info & Appearance," and then select "Sections" from the menu at the top of the page:

A shop sections dialogue box will now show on your screen where you can choose your sections. Below is an illustration of the sections I chose to add, and naturally my first choice is "Sea Glass Jewelry," as these are the first keywords I want the search engines to scan:

Once you've filled out the sections and listed items under each section, they'll appear on your main Etsy page.

This has a twofold benefit: it not only improves the SEO for your shop; it also makes customers' lives a lot easier if they want to search through your shop for specific items.

Other areas where you should ensure you include your keywords are in the titles, descriptions, and tags of your listings, although these areas are covered in more detail in future chapters.

Beware of Keyword Stuffing!

By using your keywords up front in a few of your listing titles, as well as descriptions and tags, you help to optimize your shop for your chosen phrase. However, you need to keep this balanced; overuse of a phrase can be seen as "keyword stuffing." In extreme cases, the search engines have been known to penalize Web sites for abusing their system by giving them a lower ranking.

So as tempting as it can be to use your keywords as often as possible, it's better to use them moderately, and this is easily done by writing unique, enticing, and balanced descriptions that read well for the customer and are liberally peppered with your keywords.

ACTION STEPS

- Ensure your keywords are contained in your title tag, shop announcement, and shop sections.
- Include your keywords in a few of your listing titles and in the first few words of your descriptions (taking care to avoid keyword "stuffing").

Your Etsy Banner

3

YOUR BANNER is the virtual equivalent of the shop signs you find outside retail stores, and when you consider the amount of time and money that corporations and main-street shops spend on their logos and branding, it's clear that this is a key area of significance. Likewise, the banner you choose for your Etsy shop needs to both be eye-catching and convey a sense of professionalism.

Occasionally I see Etsy shops that don't make use of a banner at all. This can lead to their shops looking a little "flat," and it's definitely a missed opportunity to attract the interest of potential buyers by building anticipation and catching their attention.

A good banner really stands out on the page. As well as being eye-catching, it may feature items that the seller has created, but ideally it will always be relevant to your shop, simple, and uncluttered.

Very involved banners, with an assortment of strange colors, shapes, and abstract designs, can be effective if you're selling contemporary abstract art, but if you're selling traditional jewelry or knitwear then it could be slightly confusing for the shopper. Think of your banner as part of your brand.

Common mistakes with a poorly designed banner include blurred photographs and a clunky font with the shop name stretched, distorted, or even disappearing over the edge of the banner.

If you're disappointed with your banner or don't have one yet, then don't worry as it's easily fixed! There are some terrific designers on Etsy who sell banners, or you can create your own.

Buying a Banner

To find someone who will create your banner for you, run a search on Etsy:

You can find a number of creative, professional designers who will design a banner for you for a reasonable price.

You can also buy ready-made banners, and while these are often cheaper, bear in mind that other Etsy shops may also use the same design. If you have a little money, then it could be worth spending to have something absolutely unique created for your shop.

If you're going to buy a banner, you should also ask for an avatar, which is the small graphic that appears by your username when you send a conversation ("convo" in Etsy language) or comment on the forums within Etsy. You can usually find designers who offer packages that include banner, avatar, and business card designs, which can save a lot of time and effort and add to your business branding.

Another place where you can discover a range of designers is a Web site called fiverr, which has offers for all sorts of online work, and all for the princely sum of $5! You should take time to check feedback before hiring and you can also send e-mails asking to see samples of their work. You can find out more by visiting:

www.fiverr.com/

THE DIY BANNER

If you have experience and own photo-editing software such as Adobe Photoshop, then you should be able to make a banner in no time at all.

If you don't own Photoshop, then there is an excellent free and open-source alternative called GIMP (which stands for GNU Image Manipulation Program) at www.gimp.org, and not only is the price very reasonable (as in free), but there's plenty of support and forums where you can find an abundance of knowledge and help.

One drawback with programs such as Photoshop and GIMP is that they carry a steep learning curve. It can take months or even years of exploration to become familiar with the vast array of tools they offer.

Thankfully, there's a fantastic simple and free alternative you can use called pixlr:

www.pixlr.com/

This is an online service, which means you don't need to download software and you can create your banner or upload and edit images online.

IDEAS

A great way to start the design process is by gathering ideas. If you are feeling stuck, start by creating a simple banner that includes your Etsy shop name and a one-line phrase summarizing your art or craft. For instance, my Etsy shop might have the shop name "Sea Glass Jewelry Box" and my "one-line phrase" below might be "Sparkling Jewels Shaped by the Sea."

If you want to develop ideas for designing your banner, looking at examples can help to get the creative juices flowing. You can take a look at some of Etsy's top sellers by using the ever-helpful Craft Count.

www.craftcount.com

As you look through the top results, make a note of their banners (taking a moment to analyze the photography and how items are listed can also be highly informative). Is it eye-catching? Are they using a clear and vibrant font?

Does it represent their items, brand, or style? Would it encourage someone to browse through their shops? These are the targets that we want to hit when it comes to a well-designed banner.

MAKING A BANNER ON PIXLR

I'm going to make a banner on pixlr for my imaginary Etsy shop so that you can see all the steps.

First, head on over to pixlr at:

www.pixlr.com/

You can either create a brand-new image yourself or make your banner using the theme of your Etsy shop, which is the option I'm going to choose for this example.

First, select "Open image editor":

Then click on "Create a new image":

Etsy recommends that your banner measures 760 pixels wide by 100 pixels high, so this is the image size that you need to type into pixlr:

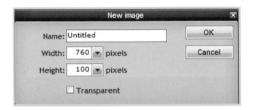

Now you have a blank white canvas to work with:

At this stage, you could play around with colors and fonts and create a banner from scratch, but I'm going to use an image from my computer. To do this, go to the top of the menu on pixlr and select "File," then "Open":

Now you need to navigate to the folder on your computer and find the photograph you'll be working with.

In this instance I have a photograph from the beach with a selection of stones, which ties in with the beach theme for my sample sea glass jewelry shop.

Once you've opened the image you want to use, you need to select it. You can do this either by clicking "Control" and "A" on your keyboard or going to the menu and selecting "Edit," then "Select all":

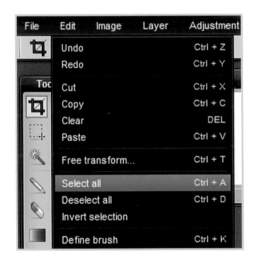

Now that your image is selected, you'll see dashed lines, sometimes referred to as "running ants," surrounding your image.

To copy either press "Control" and "C" or select "Edit" from the menu and click "Copy."

Then navigate back to the blank banner you made a moment ago and press "Control" and "V", or select "Edit" from the menu and then "Paste."

Once your picture has been pasted into your banner, you'll probably want to reposition it. In my example I want to shrink the picture because for now it's too large:

You can shrink your image by enlarging the canvas you're working on, which will make the transformation process easier.

To do this, click and drag the field in the bottom right-hand corner as shown below:

Now it's time to transform the image. I want to resize mine, so I can either go to "Edit" and click on "Free Transform" or click "Control" (or "Command" for Macs) and "T".

In free-transform mode you'll see an outline around your picture and a small square box, which you can then drag and drop until it's in the position that best works for you. You need to hold down the Shift key on your keyboard as you re-size, in order to keep your picture from warping.

Once you've shrunk your image, you can click off the corner box and then click anywhere within the picture to drag and drop it around the screen until it's in the best position.

When you're happy with the placement of your image, simply press "Enter" or "Return" on your keyboard.

Now that I have the base for my banner, it's time to add text.

You can access the "type" tool on the left-hand "Tools" sidebar either by pressing "T" on your keyboard or by selecting it as shown below:

Once you've selected the "type" tool, click on your banner and a text dialogue box will open:

Whatever you type in this box appears on a new layer over your banner. As you can see, there are several options and a drop-down where you can change your font, size, style, and color.

You can also drag the type around and position it by pressing "V" or selecting the "Move" tool from the Tools menu:

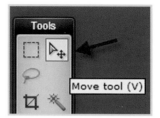

Something to watch out for is that you're moving your "type" layer and not your background image. You can check which layer is active (and therefore the one you're working on) by looking at the Layers palette on the right-hand side of the screen:

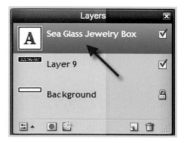

From the above illustration you can see the active layer is highlighted in blue. In this example, my

"Text Layer" is active and below is "Layer 1" and if I want to switch to this layer and make any edits I simply click on the layer and ensure it's highlighted. I can now drag and move the text around until it's in the correct position and nudge it using the cursor (arrow) keys on my keyboard until it's centered:

Depending on your personal preferences and the image you're working with, you can place the text wherever it looks best. I don't always center text; sometimes it can make images look dull or flat, but for this image, centered seemed to work best.

Now the final step is to save your image so that you can upload it to Etsy.

To do this, go to the top menu, "File" and "Save," or click "Control" and S":

In the Save Box, you will need to name your file. I've called mine Sea Glass Jewelry. You can then select the option "Save to my computer" (see image below), choose JPEG format, and I upped the "Quality" to 100, for the best file quality possible.

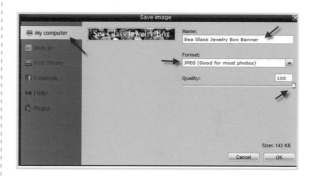

You now have a brand-new banner for your Etsy shop! Here's how to upload it:

Go back to "Your Etsy," "Shop Settings," and click on "Info & Appearance":

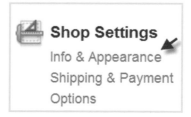

The right-hand side of the page is the location to upload your new banner:

Now browse to the location on your computer where you saved your banner in pixlr, highlight the file name, and click "Save Changes" at the foot of the page in Etsy.

To see your new banner, click on "Shop" at the top of the screen:

Your new banner should now be showing. The last part of this exercise is to make an avatar for your shop.

Avatar

Your avatar is a small graphic that shows whenever you log in to Etsy and participate on the site, for instance when you post in the forums or add an Etsy shop to your "favorites" (more on this later). Your avatar is a valuable opportunity to pique interest in your shop.

Some people make their avatar a portrait of themselves, and this can be an effective way to highlight the personal nature of Etsy as a handmade marketplace. Customers often like to see the person they're buying from, so this also helps build trust with the buyer.

Another option is for a simple eye-catching graphic, clear and bright, and possibly your "signature" creation. Just as a chef has a signature dish, which people associate with their food, perhaps you have an item that neatly summarizes your creations and emphasizes your brand?

In this example I'm going to use a piece of sea glass jewelry, and while it may look a little abstract, I hope it will look compelling enough for someone to want to click on.

So revisit pixlr and click on "Open image editor" and "Create new image." You'll need to set the size of the canvas for your avatar to 75 pixels wide by 75 pixels high (which are the dimensions Etsy recommends):

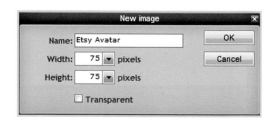

Now that I have a blank canvas, I'm going to drag the image I want to use as an avatar onto the canvas.

This is the same process as when you opened an image for your banner. You need to go to the top of the menu, click on "File," then "Open," select an image from your computer, and press "Control" and "A" or click on "Edit" and "Select all."

Once your image is selected and the "running ants" are showing, paste it into your new canvas and resize and reshape it:

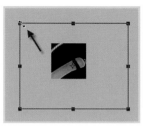

So now I save the above avatar to my computer as before and upload it to Etsy.

To do this you need to go to "Your Etsy" and then "Profile":

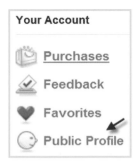

In the center of the page, you'll see a box (as below). Simply click on "Browse" and navigate to the avatar you saved on your computer.

Now scroll down to the bottom of the page and click "Save Changes."

Now you have a brand-new banner and avatar!

Using pixlr is fun, so experiment! It's certainly worthwhile to create several banners and avatars that utilize different ideas or variations on your theme. Comparing your designs side by side can be really helpful when it comes to deciding which is most effective, and you could also get second opinions from friends, family, or fellow Etsy sellers on the forums.

ACTION STEPS

- Decide whether to outsource your banner design or create it yourself.

- Examine the top Etsy sellers and see how their banners have been designed.

- Make sure your banner looks both professional as well as eye-catching and rank it honestly on a scale of 1 to 10. Ask on the forums for an honest appraisal to discover possible ways of making improvements.

- Acquire an avatar as well as a banner and try to ensure the designs have a similarity that will be both unique and recognizable as belonging to your shop.

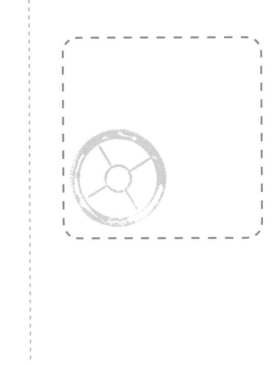

Writing Listings That Sell

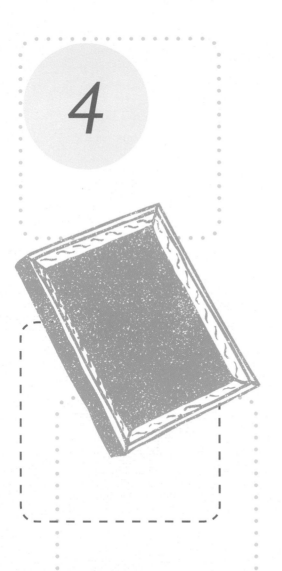

4

THE WAY you construct and write your listings is of key importance for two reasons. First, the text within your listings is another area where the search engines scan to find relevant keywords. Second, after your photography the copy is the next place where you get a chance to hook the viewers' attention and hopefully give them an extra nudge towards making a purchase.

So what makes a well-written listing?

Here's an example of a perfectly good advertisement, which lists all of the features of the item it's selling but doesn't really *sell*:

SEA GLASS JEWELRY BOX PENDANT

This listing is for a Green Sea Glass Pendant with a sterling silver bail and 16-inch sterling silver box chain.

This would make a fantastic gift for someone special!

Technically there's nothing wrong with this text. It gets to the point and you know exactly what you'll be receiving, as well as the measurements of the chain. It describes the item perfectly, but the potential customer can get most of these facts by looking at the photograph.

When it comes to buying, people don't want to just learn about the features; they want to know how they'll benefit from their purchases, how owning an item will make them feel. In short, people often base their buying decisions around emotions and benefits rather than features and facts.

When you write copy for your listings, you should strive to tell a story and to engage your visitors on an emotional level.

Three Steps

I use three steps when it comes to writing an advertisement. Each step provides a framework and can make writing sales copy nice and simple:

1. Tell them what you have.
2. Tell them what it will do for them.
3. Finally, tell them what they need to do next.

So here's an example of how I'd improve the above listing in order to engage the reader and, I hope, turn a casual window-shopper into an eager buyer:

GORGEOUS BOTTLE GREEN SEA GLASS JEWELRY BOX PENDANT

A divine deep green Sea Glass Pendant, which glistens and shines as if it were washed up on a sun-drenched shore.

This simple yet elegant piece of Sea Glass Jewelry is not only completely unique, but the glass has been left as found and is therefore wholly natural—one of Mother Nature's bounties sure to catch people's eyes with its delicate beauty!

When you buy this pendant you also receive a 16-inch sterling silver box chain, and if you need this adjusted to a different length please contact me; I'm always happy to help!

This is a one-of-a-kind [*or you could mention "limited-edition"*] piece of highly distinctive jewelry, sure to complement your style. Add this wearable art to your cart now before someone else snaps up this delightful treasure!

I'm sure you can see the difference between the two listings. The first description is matter-of-fact and seems almost ashamed to sell itself, while the second one is rich in imagery that will help people to conjure up pictures in their mind's eye. Engaging people's imaginations is very powerful when it comes to selling. The final paragraph tells people to "add to your cart" and how not doing so may lead them to disappointment and losing out on owning a one-of-a-kind piece of jewelry (scarcity can be a powerfully motivating force!).

The conclusion of the listing is telling people to take action *now*.

There's no guarantee that people will make the purchase after reading the second listing, but I hope you can see that it's a lot more seductive and appealing to paint a picture with words, rather than simply listing an item's materials and measurements.

It can often be really helpful to include a line or two about how you came up with the idea for your creations or where you found the materials, if this is a point of interest. This can add to the story and help the reader connect with you as a person.

Another important point when writing any form of copy is to try to break it down into short paragraphs. People often feel overwhelmed because there are so many descriptions and different forms of media competing for their attention. If you deliver your information in short paragraphs, it makes reading and digesting copy far easier.

It's also a good idea to ensure your copy contains correct *spelling*. It only takes a few moments to check your spelling, whether through text-editing software on your computer or an online "spell-checker." While many people's perceptions of spelling and grammar are changing with the advent of texting and e-mail, a well-written and grammatically correct listing lends an air of professionalism and attention to detail.

Finally, you should never be afraid to *sell*. You've put hours of hard work into your creations—in the crafting, the sourcing of materials, and imagining new designs. You've literally created something that wasn't there before, which is a huge achievement, so don't be afraid to sell it!

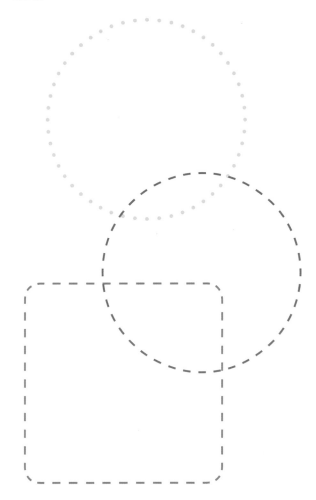

ACTION STEPS

Read through your Etsy listings. Do they:

- ☐ Include your keywords?
- ☐ Describe benefits over features?
- ☐ Engage the reader's emotions?
- ☐ Contain a call to action?
- ☐ Tell a story or provide an interesting fact?
- ☐ Have reader-friendly text with short paragraphs rather than lengthy blocks of copy or overwhelming chunks with "too much information"?
- ☐ Have correct spelling and grammar?

A Crash Course in Photography

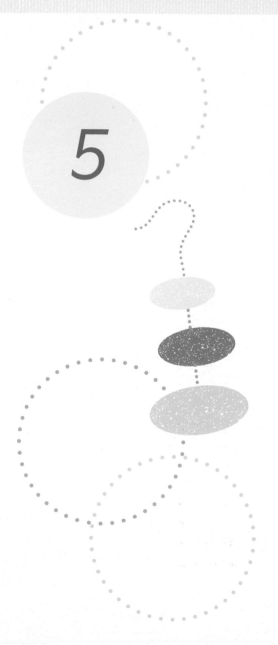

5

GOOD PHOTOGRAPHY is absolutely key to selling online; it can mean the difference between capturing potential customers' attention and losing them completely! Customers can click away from your page in an instant, so you want to do your best to tempt them to browse and buy from your shop. Beautiful pictures make a great first impression, communicate clearly, and can motivate interested shoppers.

Communicating Through Your Images

A picture is worth a thousand words, so really think about what your images are saying. Selling online is complicated by the fact that customers can't hold or examine the item that they're interested in and there's no salesperson to refer to for immediate answers. Your images can answer so many questions; the more clear and concise information you can provide with your images the better! If customers can't find the answers they're looking for within your listing, they may not buy. Sending a conversation through Etsy and waiting for the answer takes time; customers in the mood for an impulse purchase may just decide to move on.

Each listing on Etsy provides space for up to five images. This is a golden opportunity!

Here are the five images you should provide:

1. The "Attention Grabber": You really want your first image to grab the viewers' interest, and a high-quality image is vital; zooming in or cropping can add interest. Experiment!
2. Details: Provide close-up shots or full shots that reveal and show the details that may be relevant to the buyers, like the clasp on a necklace or the buttons on a sweater.
3. Details—Back or side angles: Since your customers can't turn the piece over, do it for them. They may wish to understand how a piece has been finished on the back or sides, so this is where you can show them and answer a question before it arises.
4. Details—Scale: a shot of your item modeled, displayed on graph paper with a ruler or common object like a pencil or coin, can help your customers better understand the dimensions of the piece visually.
5. Additional Information: If you feel you've expressed all that you can with your first four images, this fifth slot can be utilized with a graphic that reminds your customers of a helpful fact like "I love making custom orders," "Express shipping available," or, "For more great jewelry have a look in my shop!"

Troubleshooting

Occasionally I'll see amazing and wholly original creations while shopping online, but, sadly, a lot of them may go completely unnoticed because they're poorly photographed. Images that are dark, blurry, shadowy, washed out, or taken against a "busy" background can be unappealing, distracting, overlooked, or even confusing as to what is on offer. Bad photography can really work against you, and as sellers we need to address these potential issues and look at our images objectively.

Lighting

Diffused daylight is considered best for photography because it eliminates shadows, resulting in clean, clear images. You can get very good results photographing your items by a bright, indirectly lit window or outdoors on an overcast day, but I have found that waiting for the perfect natural lighting is not always convenient.

This is why I prefer using a lightbox (more on this in a moment) lit with daylight compact fluorescent bulbs. With this setup you can photograph your items at any time of the day or night and achieve consistent, professional results. Daylight bulbs are fantastic for photography because they keep the lighting pure, producing a whiter, more natural light than standard incandescent bulbs, and help to keep colors true.

Before I began to use daylight bulbs, my photographs were inconsistent and at times they had a strange blue tinge. This was because I was using different types of bulbs, one incandescent and two tungsten at the same time. Each bulb was burning at a different "light temperature," which was adversely affecting my photographs.

Investing in daylight bulbs for your photography can really improve your images and save valuable time. Purchase the highest wattage you can afford. I suggest a minimum of 30 watts, which is about the highest you can get at your local hardware store (and equal to about 125 watts from standard lightbulbs). Higher-wattage bulbs are available online from shops that specialize in photography supplies.

Proper lighting can really improve your photography, because photographs taken in poorly lit rooms can be blurry, washed out, dull, or muddy. With so many variables, it may take some time and experimentation to find the best setup for your environment and equipment.

Tripod

A tripod is a fantastic tool; it's like having an extra set of steady hands! In addition to poor lighting, one of the ways that photographs can end up blurred is if there is the slightest camera movement as the photograph is being taken. Using a tripod solves this issue, and once set up, a tripod makes taking your photos a snap!

You really don't need to spend a fortune; you can find a number of inexpensive or secondhand tripods for under $20. If you're photographing smaller items in a lightbox, then a simple "mini-tripod" may be all you need.

Lightbox

A lightbox is like a miniature photography studio where you can photograph your subject in beautiful diffused light with the background of your choice and get terrific and consistent results. There are many different sizes and models available for purchase, or you can make your own simple and effective lightbox for next to nothing. A quick online search will result in plenty of free tutorials.

Below is a picture of a pair of earrings taken in a lightbox. As you can see, the earrings are the focal point of the photograph and, while the background may be plain, it helps to keep the viewer's focus where it needs to be, i.e., on the jewelry:

This image still needs some editing, which will be covered later in this chapter, but I hope you can see the benefits of using a lightbox; it draws the viewer to the earrings, with nothing else to distract attention away from the jewelry.

Below is a picture of the same earrings in a different setting to illustrate the difference that using a lightbox can make:

At first glance would you know this listing is for a pair of earrings? With the thumbnail photo making the initial impression, a customer might think the listing was for a teacup and find themselves disappointed that it's not the item being advertised. While the teacup is ornate and looks nice, it really doesn't serve the earrings. This is because the earrings aren't the focal point of the photograph and my attention is not immediately drawn to the jewelry. Artful use of props and scenery can be very effective in selling, but you want to be sure that they *quietly* complement your items and do not overwhelm them.

Control the Shot

Choose props and backgrounds carefully; consider everything that will show in your images, and avoid clutter and distraction. The use of a lightbox gives you maximum control over the shot because the only focal point for the camera is the subject in view. When executed with skill and care, scenery can be really eye-catching, but I prefer photographing on a plain card stock, because it's simple and effective when it comes to focusing attention on my subject.

You can experiment with colored and patterned backdrops and brand your Etsy shop through your photography by developing a sense of uniformity with your images. If you stick with a simple recognizable style or background, it can lend a sense of consistency to your shop and help to make your listings easily identifiable to people browsing on Etsy.

But what if you're photographing items that are too large for a lightbox?

Sometimes photographing outdoors or in a bright room might be your best solution, but when taking photographs you always need to consider the background and how it might add to or subtract from your purpose. For example, taking photographs in your backyard has the potential to produce images that may be distracting to the viewer. People might instinctively work out the main subject matter, but clutter can quickly lead the eye away from your focal point. Do your best to control everything that is within the camera frame and set up your shots carefully.

Backdrops are a very effective remedy; a simple makeshift backdrop can be made with a sheet or length of fabric.

Camera Settings

Many digital cameras are designed for people to use straight out of the box, which, while convenient, can hold drawbacks. People often skim through the accompanying manuals so they can start playing with their new gadget as soon as possible, but the preset options on digital cameras are not necessarily configured for the best performance when you need to take specific shots. It is important to understand how your specific camera works and what adjustments can be made to ensure that your pictures are the best they can be.

A setting that you should always check is image size. Often cameras will be preset to take smaller-sized photographs; this is so you can fit as many photographs onto the memory card as possible, which is fine if you're taking snapshots for fun, but for photographing your Etsy creations you need the highest possible file size.

Essentially, the larger the file sizes, the more detail the camera captures. By making this adjustment you will have a higher-quality image to work with when it comes to editing for color and cropping your images. Your post-processed photographs will also be larger, giving visitors on Etsy the ability to click and zoom to see more detail.

Because I know that I can always downsize my photos later if necessary, I have my camera on the highest-quality setting to ensure that I take the best possible photographs and I invested in a second memory card to ensure I always have extra memory.

Color Balance

Once your photographs are ready you'll need to do a little post-processing work to get the most from them. The photo-editing software available today is fantastic—I love Photoshop—but if you don't own editing software, no problem! Picnik is an amazing and completely free online service, which will allow you to adjust colors, sharpness, brightness, and file size, as well as cropping your images.

You can visit Picnik at:

www.picnik.com/

Click on "Get started now!"

Once Picnik has loaded, click on "Upload a photo". Now you need to navigate to the folder where you store your Etsy photographs, select a file, and click "Open." Your image should now be showing in Picnik. There are plenty of choices to work with within Picnik including "Autofix," "Crop," and "Colors." It's worth taking the time to to familiarize yourself with each of these as each function offers a way for you to improve your photography.

If you're stretched for time or just want to get an idea of what Picnik can do, click on the "Auto-fix" button, which is the first option on the left (below home).

The following image is before "Auto-fix":

And after:

As you can see, the second picture is lighter and the colors more pronounced and the image has also been sharpened.

You can make these adjustments manually, and if at any point you want to undo an adjustment or redo a change, you can use the buttons on the right-hand side of the interface:

Here's the result of the changes I made to my photograph after using the various options within Picnik:

First I used "Auto-fix"; then I adjusted the "Exposure" and "Color" and then used "Sharpen" to make a clearer and more colorful picture.

Each photograph you upload will be different, so there's no specific formula; it really does come down to trial and error.

Once you've made your adjustments, you need to save your picture. You can do this by clicking on the "Save & Share" tab at the top of the interface:

The share options above the photograph offer plenty of places you can send your image, including Facebook, Twitter, and Flickr, which is a really handy feature if you want to post your image online.

But, for this exercise, I'm going to save to my PC so that I can upload to Etsy. Three points to consider are:

1. Your "file name": it's best to give your image a new name before you save, to avoid over-writing your original photograph.
2. When it comes to format, I leave it at JPG, as this is perfect for uploading to Etsy.
3. The next option that is really important is JPG compression, which I drag to the far right (10)—this means you're saving at optimal size, which will give your customers the best preview when they click on your images.

Last, click "Save Photo" and you're done!

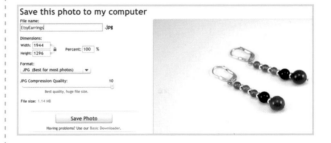

Once you get the hang of Picnik, editing and improving your images will become a fast and simple task.

Watermarks

Some photographers and artists use watermarks in their pictures to protect their work. This is understandable, because if you upload a large image, anyone can click on the preview picture and download and print it.

I find watermarks off-putting when they're spread across an image, and they can be a distraction from the art. This can be avoided by uploading a lower-resolution image, which will look great online but if printed will come out at a really low quality.

You can achieve this quickly and easily within Picnik. Simply click on "Upload a photo" on the front page and select the image from your com-

puter. Then click on the "Save & Share" tab, rename your image—for instance, if my image was called Beach Stones, I would call it Beach Stones reduced—and then lower the JPG Compression

Quality to at least halfway down the slider (as you can see, I reduced mine to 5):

This will provide you with an acceptably sized image for preview on Etsy, but cannot be printed at a decent resolution, and it is a great way to safeguard your work while offering people a clear preview.

The quality of previews you offer of your work is incredibly important. I suggest taking some time to look through your shop and then take a look at other shops on Etsy and honestly ask yourself if your photography is up to snuff.

Pictures taken with thought, care, and attention to detail will not only showcase your beautiful creations in the best possible way; they also will go a long way towards conveying that you care deeply about your craft and take your business and customers seriously. With practice, patience, and experimentation you can dramatically improve the quality of your images and the appearance of your Etsy shop.

ACTION STEPS

Ensure your photographs are:

- ☐ Well lit
- ☐ In focus
- ☐ The center of attention (no clutter!)
- ☐ The highest file size possible for your camera
- ☐ Optimized in Picnik or with photo-editing software to ensure the colors stand out

The Art of Tagging

6

TAGS are keywords that describe the information contained on a Web page. When you make a search on Etsy for an item, these tags will enable Etsy's search engine to return relevant listings.

Each Etsy listing has a space for fourteen tags, offering you fourteen opportunities to bring people to your shop—and each one counts!

Coming up with fourteen different tags for your items can take some time and thought, but it's worth sitting down with a pen and paper to work through some phrases that people might use to find the types of items you're creating.

A few minutes spent brainstorming should help you fill in any blanks. Once you've got your first fourteen tags, you may find them useful for many of your other listings, especially if your shop has a certain theme. Saving a "master list" on Etsy makes filling out the tags for future items a lot quicker and easier, and this will evolve over time as you add new items to your shop.

Going back to my sea glass jewelry pendant example, at first glance there are three obvious tags to start with: "sea glass," "green," and "pendant."

"Sea glass" is my primary phrase, but it's also possible that some people will type in "seaglass" with no space. Another example where you may use a similar tag twice is "jewelry" (the American spelling) and "jewellery" (the British spelling). Allowing for variations like these, even if they could be considered misspelled, is something to consider, and by using both variations you help maximize your visibility.

After a quick brainstorm, I have come up with over fourteen tags that might be good choices for my listing:

sea glass, seaglass, beach glass, beachglass, pendant, charm, necklace, aqua, naturally formed, sea, ocean, silver, up-cycled, green, eco friendly, wire wrapped, jewelry, jewellery

Using a specific keyword once in the title, tags, or materials is enough, so I will choose the tags from my list bearing this in mind.

For example, if my listing title is "Sea Glass Jewelry Pendant," I would not need to use the words "sea glass," "jewelry," or "pendant" in my tags.

Colors

Colors make great tags for people who may be shopping for an item in a particular color. Sometimes the sheer range of options available in Etsy can be a little overwhelming and, to narrow the lists down, some people might add a color to their search. So, for my example, the tags "aqua" and "silver" might be good choices.

The terms "sea," "ocean," and "aqua" are good descriptive tags that illustrate the piece and could help people shopping for a certain theme.

Tag Your Shop Name

It can be effective to use your shop name as a tag in some of your listings. The Etsy search function defaults to "handmade items," and unless your shop name is in the title or tags of some of your listings, a search on your shop name will show zero results, frustrating anyone who might be trying to find you.

Trends

Another idea to come up with tags for your items is by watching upcoming trends on Etsy, which you can often find by keeping an eye on the Etsy forums or the news or by using Google trends:

www.google.com/trends

If you find a phrase that relates to your work and it's a rising trend, then this can be a good way to increase your visitors.

You want to be careful that the terms you use are relevant to your items; using a tag simply because it's popular is more likely to annoy and frustrate a buyer than it is to help you make a sale.

By making sure that your tags are on target you help people find exactly what they're looking for, and this could increase the chances of making that sale.

ACTION STEPS

Ensure you are:

- ☐ Using *all* fourteen tags
- ☐ Including *all* spellings to attract international shoppers (i.e., "jewellery" as well as "jewelry")
- ☐ Using colors within your tags
- ☐ Using your shop name as one of your tags

Profiling You

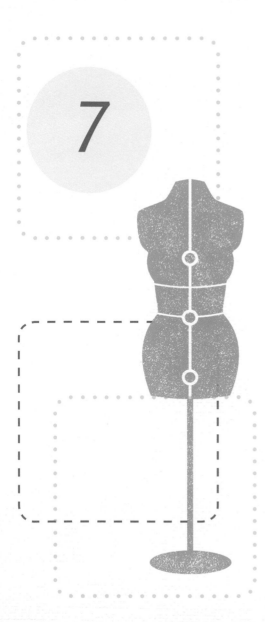

7

THE PROFILE area of your Etsy shop is an excellent opportunity to connect with your customers by including a little information about yourself: how you developed your skills and what inspires you to create. People like to know who they're buying from in the same way that they might read a bio or seek further information about a musician or author they admire; it helps to paint a fuller picture.

When it comes to your profile, rather than talking up the benefits of buying an item in your shop, you're selling yourself as an artist and creator. Enthusiasm can be infectious, and the more you can convey the excitement and passion you have for your work, the more interested the reader will become.

To access your profile, sign in to Etsy and click on "Public Profile."

A good way to start off your profile is with a short bio; think of it as an interview and write responses to questions that someone might want to ask you. How long have you been making————? What inspires you? What is it that you love about making———? What's the most rewarding aspect of your work?

Interesting Points

Perhaps there are some interesting key points to your work, exotic ingredients or interesting materials, or historical facts? Tell people!

Talk about places where your work has been featured, for instance, Web sites or galleries, or perhaps you've won awards or prizes? Including this information can intrigue the reader, and the more you connect with your audience, the more trust and confidence you can build in the buyer.

Etsy shops are the opposite of faceless multinationals. They are designed to be friendly and personal spaces; the farmers' market versus the supermarket, a place where buyers and artists can interact. If you ensure your profile is warm and approachable, you may increase your chances of receiving conversations from eager buyers. It's like leaving a virtual door open for people to pop their head round and say hi! If you're happy to make custom orders, mentioning this can also invite inquiries that can lead to sales.

It's best to try to keep your profile as concise as possible. People can often be overwhelmed by large blocks of text, and one way to minimize this is by breaking the information down into short paragraphs.

Your profile is also the place where you should disclose any other Etsy shops or usernames that you utilize. You can simply say "I am also on Etsy" as "username" or you can provide a link to the URL.

Once you've written your profile, consider e-mailing the link to friends and family for a second opinion, or post it in the Etsy forums, asking for a shared critique. It's always a good idea to get a second opinion, and being open-minded with thoughts and suggestions can ensure your profile is as effective as possible.

ACTION STEPS

Does your profile:

- ☐ Come off as warm and friendly?
- ☐ Convey enthusiasm?
- ☐ Include any interesting or notable facts?
- ☐ Read easily?
- ☐ Disclose any other Etsy shops that you may own?

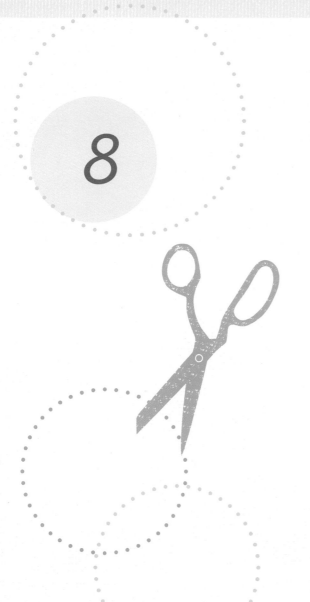

Google E-mail

WHEN YOU first set up your Etsy account, you will have to provide an e-mail address. This can be changed at any time within "Account" under "Your Account." The e-mail address that you provide is really important because this is how you receive notifications about your account, such as when you make a sale or receive a conversation on Etsy or when it's time to pay your Etsy bill.

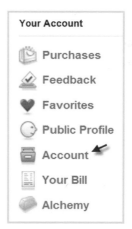

You may be tempted to use your personal e-mail address, but in terms of keeping everything organized I highly recommend you set up a new e-mail address that is dedicated to your Etsy shop and shop business. I find it's really helpful to keep everything in one place, separate from personal messages and easily accessible should I need to go back and check through my sales history when questions arise. You can still receive copies of e-mails to your personal e-mail address by having messages automatically forwarded by your e-mail provider. This is easy to set up, and later on in this chapter I will show you how.

I find Gmail (or Google Mail) the best e-mail client for organization and search capabilities, which can save lots of time when you need to find and refer to an older e-mail!

If you prefer using Hotmail or Yahoo! then it may be better to stick with what works best for you, but you will still need a Gmail account to access a lot of the resources that are shared in later chapters. If you decide to set up a new Gmail account that is connected to your shop, I recommend you use your Etsy shop name, because this is the e-mail address that will show up on your customers' sales receipts when you begin to make sales.

To sign up for a new Gmail account, visit:

mail.google.com/mail/signup

or type "Gmail" into your Web browser.

If the e-mail address you wish to use has already been taken, you can try adding a short phrase or couple of digits to the end. For in-stance, if seaglassjewelrybox@gmail.com is not available, try seaglassjewelryshop@gmail.com or seaglassjewelry77@gmail.com.

Here are some of the great benefits to using Gmail.

Space

At the time of writing, when you sign up for Gmail you receive more than 7GB of space, which equates to a lot of e-mail messages, and this allotted space is continuously increasing. Space can become an issue over time; personal e-mail accounts fill up and become unable to accept new messages. This is unlikely to occur with a Gmail account solely for Etsy messages because your e-mails are unlikely to contain large attachments.

Unless you delete an e-mail it remains in Gmail for the life span of your account, which really helps in terms of keeping a detailed history of your transactions and communications. Google is an established company that invests heavily in servers, security, and new technologies. While Gmail has excellent security, backing up your records is always a good idea.

Finding information within your account is easy with the Gmail search function. It works exactly the same way as a Google search, so if you received an Etsy conversation from someone requesting a custom item and couldn't quite remember who they were or when it was sent, by typing the word "custom" into the Gmail "search mail" box you will get a return result with all the e-mails that contain this word or phrase. This alone can save a huge amount of time and frustration, and because Gmail keeps all of the e-mails that you both send and receive (unless you choose to delete messages) you will have a constant record of your communications. This becomes useful if you have any inquiries or a dispute, which is why I recommend you keep all Etsy shop e-mails and business communications for future reference.

Organization

Gmail is smart; as you type an e-mail Gmail automatically saves it as a draft. This is a lifesaving feature, which many of the older e-mail providers failed to provide. Have you ever lost an entire e-mail that took ages to write? *Frustrating*, to say the least! If you lose your Internet connection while typing an e-mail within Gmail, usually when you return to your Gmail account you will find an up-to-date draft waiting to be finished and sent.

Another great organizational feature is Google Calendar, which you can use in conjunction with your Gmail to see reminders of important tasks; this can be invaluable when you're running a business.

You can also make use of Google Docs, which includes spreadsheets and word-processing soft-

ware, and these can be sent and shared with other Google account users no matter if they utilize a Mac or PC.

Forwarding Your Business E-mail Automatically

If you want to have messages sent from your Etsy shop's Gmail account to your personal e-mail (which can be handy if you want to be kept up-to-date with new sales and Etsy conversations), you can do so by clicking on "Settings" in your Gmail account.

In the "Settings" menu, click on "Forwarding and POP/IMAP" and then "Add a forwarding address," as shown below:

You can now enter your personal e-mail address where you want your Etsy Gmail messages to be forwarded to. Once you click "submit," you will need to sign in to your personal e-mail to collect a verification code. Copy this code, sign back in to your Etsy shop's Gmail account, and paste in the code in "Settings," "Forwarding and POP/IMAP," "Forwarding," and "Verify."

To reverse this at any point, simply return to "Settings" and "Forwarding and POP/IMAP" and click on "Remove Address."

There are masses of extras that come with Gmail and it's worth taking some time to explore them, but something that will definitely be relevant later in this book is Google Places and You-Tube (both owned by Google), excellent services for increasing visibility of your business. To use these you will need a Google account, but if you prefer a different e-mail client, it's still a good idea to sign up for a free Google account to use these services.

Your E-mail Signature

Gmail allows you to use an e-mail signature, a short message that will appear at the bottom of each e-mail you send. Adding and updating messages in your signature, which include a link to your shop, is another great marketing opportunity.

To add a signature, go back to your Gmail settings and click on "General":

Approximately halfway down the page is a box to add your signature:

As you can see from my example, I've added a brief note and links to my Etsy shop and Twitter address (more on Twitter later). Now each time I send out an e-mail, I also send a little reminder and links that inform people about my business.

You can put whatever you like in this space, but it's best to keep your message brief. Using a PS message can be a good way to increase click-through, as people's eyes are often drawn to the PS messages that follow as additional brief snippets of information after your signature, for example:

For unique and unusual jewelry designs, click: seaglassjewelrybox.etsy.com

If you can think of a fun or intriguing message to add to your signature, it's another potential way to share your Web site through viral marketing—especially if you send out the sort of e-mail that people are likely to want to forward on to their friends, such as funny, cute, bizarre, or informative You-Tube videos or links to interesting Web sites.

ACTION STEPS

- Open a Gmail account using your Etsy shop name (or a close match if this is unavailable).

- Create an e-mail signature with your Etsy shop URL, together with a brief and engaging message.

- Experiment with Google Calendar in conjuction with Google Mail to note important events, such as taking stock, ordering new materials, and paying your Etsy bill.

- Set up a "Google Task" within your Gmail Acount. Google Tasks are another simple way to build and keep track of a "to-do" list.

- Become familair with Google Documents (or Google Docs) which can be accessed within Gmail under "Documents." Google Docs is a free service that allows you to create text documents, as well as spreadsheets and presentations. You can also share these documents with contacts, which is really helpful for collaborations.

Packing and Preparation

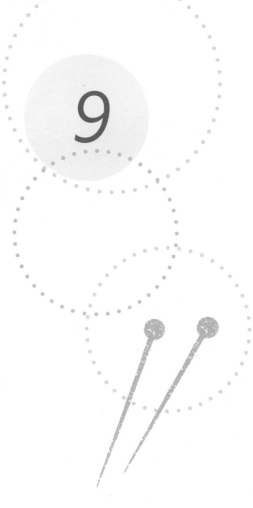

9

THIS CHAPTER may seem unnecessary because the lessons are so obvious: essentially, make sure you have plenty of packaging and be prepared for the holidays! If you're not prepared, you could end up with chaos in the run-up to the busiest seasons, which can be damaging to both creativity and sales.

When I started to apply some of the lessons in this book to my wife's jewelry shop, we were completely unprepared for the spike in holiday sales. With a combination of buyers coming from social media sites (explained in future chapters) and natural, organic pre-Christmas sales, we struggled with inventory.

Packaging

This lack of preparation led to frantically searching around for old envelopes and boxes to recycle for shipping. While recycling is important, cutting up old boxes and removing labels from envelopes during the holiday rush was adding hours to the week.

The time spent trying to make packing materials could have been better spent making new items, writing to customers, photographing creations, and listing them on Etsy. All of these are good reasons for ensuring you're prepared. You can easily avoid similar issues by stocking up with envelopes and boxes and maintaining your stock on a monthly basis.

One great place to buy affordable packaging is eBay, and if you shop around you can find some fantastic bargains. This is often a better option than buying packing materials in brick-and-mortar stores, which may happen if you're buying in "panic mode" because you've run out of supplies.

Pricing

You can factor the cost of packaging into either your item prices or your shipping totals, but setting shipping costs can sometimes be a little tricky. One way to work out the best price for shipping is to look at a cross section of other sellers and see what they're charging.

This is important because, as a buyer, I'll occasionally find an item I wish to purchase only to see a completely unreasonable shipping charge, which sometimes leads me to emptying my cart and shopping elsewhere.

By factoring the packaging charges into the item as well as the shipping, sellers can avoid their shipping charges appearing inflated. If your shipping costs are high due to materials, then it's better to add a couple of dollars onto your listing to cover costs and keep your shipping lower.

Notes

In addition to packaging, you can also buy a "return address" stamp online so you only have to stamp the outside of your packages, rather than writing your address by hand. This can save a lot of time with shipping, and it's amazing how these small jobs add up over the course of the year! Any time that is being spent on manual tasks is time missed creating new items and working on your shop.

It can be a nice touch to include a small handwritten note with your items. Etsy gives the opportunity to provide a personal touch, and customers may really appreciate a simple note thanking them for their business and wishing them all the best. These sorts of touches are why people would prefer to buy from places like Etsy rather than the chain stores, and if you reinforce this you may experience return customers.

My wife includes a small note, which reads: "Dear [first name], thank you so much for your purchase! I really hope you enjoy your [item]! All the best! [Signature]" It only takes moments to write, and people clearly appreciate the gesture, which is reflected when they leave feedback.

Feedback

Speaking of feedback, there's no reason why you shouldn't ask buyers to leave it for you. Some people frown upon this, but as long as your request is worded in a friendly way, it can really help to boost your feedback and ratings.

When you leave feedback for others, you have three extra opportunities to gain exposure for your shop. One is your avatar; if you have a strong graphic, people may notice it. You can also refer to your shop in your feedback, for instance: "Thanks so much for buying from Sea Glass Jewelry Box and for your excellent communications...." You can also include a "Customer appreciation picture," and if it's something eye-catching or intriguing it could lead to another click-through to your shop.

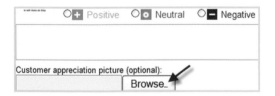

Postcard

A further way to advertise is by buying postcards printed with your logo or a really sharp picture that people would want to keep (or better yet stick on their fridge!). This graphic has to be really strong, and I'd suggest keeping your sales message subtle; if it's just a full-on advertisement, then it's unlikely people will want to display it in their home. This would be perfect for artists or photographers in particular.

If you buy adhesive labels, you can write your thank-you notes and affix them to the backs of the postcards.

I also recommend you include a business card when you ship your items.

As long as you get a good balance between self-promotion and sending people something they will genuinely enjoy as little "extras" with their items, you can keep goodwill with the customers and increase your chances of future sales.

International

As you read through the Etsy forums (as covered in a future chapter), it's clear that some sellers are uncomfortable with shipping internationally. Etsy is an international venue, so people who decide not to ship overseas may potentially be losing sales.

So far, my wife has shipped to Singapore, Italy, Taiwan, Brazil, Britain, and Romania, as well as the United States, and there have been few problems. You should charge more for international shipping, and if you sell similar items, you could always take them to your local post office and ask them for quotes, which you can then use in your shop's shipping polices.

If there are countries that have a poor reputation for items arriving (you can spot these in the Etsy forums and discussions on eBay), then you could insist on Express Mail International or another form of shipping that requires signature and proof of delivery. This can then be factored into the price of your shipping costs. As an illustration of how to set shipping costs for a specific country, I'm going to use Italy as an example (not as a comment of reliability of items arriving in Italy!). To set shipping costs, click on "Your Etsy," go to "Shop Settings," then click on "Shipping and Payment."

Now click on "Create a New Profile." First, you will need to give this new profile a name, and as per my example I would call mine Italy. Now select "Item Ships From" (which is wherever you're based); then for "Country Specific Shipping" you need to enter the country that you want to set a specific shipping cost for and click "Add." Now you can enter your shipping cost (as well as the cost if additional items are sent) and finally click "Save."

Create A New Shipping Profile Need help?

Name This Profile

Italy

Item Ships From

United States

Country Specific Shipping
Set shipping costs for individual countries.

Italy   Add

View Regional Shipping Options
Quickly set shipping costs for multiple countries in a predefined region at one time.

Ship to All Other Countries
Use this option if you wish to ship worldwide without setting shipping costs for each country or region.

The "Everywhere Else" shipping cost will be applied for all countries not listed in your Country Specific or Regional Shipping settings above.

Location		Shipping Cost	If shipped with another item
☐ Everywhere Else		$ 0.00	$ 0.00

SAVE   Cancel

Sometimes you're not allowed to send certain items or substances abroad, so it's worth checking with your local post office if you're in any doubt.

Customs

As you probably know, when you ship abroad you have to fill out a customs slip. One tip to save you time at the post office is to request some custom forms from your post office and fill them out at home. This can be a time-saver, and it can be really frustrating to be sent to the back of the line if you forget to fill out your customs forms. Another advantage to filling out your customs forms at home is that you can look up the costs of the items, as these will need to be included.

You may wish to add a small note regarding customs in your "Shipping Policies" on Etsy. For example, you may wish to include something similar to "All international orders require customs forms and these will be filled out truthfully. Any duty imposed by the country of destination is out of our control."

Taking care of some of the more repetitive jobs when it comes to shipping and packaging can save you time and frustration, as well as freeing up more time for you to create and expand your Etsy empire!

ACTION STEPS

- Prepare enough packaging materials and labels.
- Set your shipping costs both fairly and competitively.
- Purchase a stamp with your return address to save time and cut back on repetitive tasks.
- Draft a friendly note to thank customers for their purchase and increase your chances of customer loyalty.
- Create a promotional postcard to include with your shipment.
- Make sure you are keeping within the shipping laws of the country you are mailing to.
- Write a customs notice for your shop ensuring people are aware that all customs slips will be filled out honestly and accurately and that you are not liable for any extra charges.

Creating Professional Business Cards

10

IT'S AMAZING how often people will ask you what you do. Whether you're shopping, at a social function, exploring a craft fair, or in the waiting room at your doctor's office, you can often find people with a shared interest when it comes to art or creativity. If people are intrigued by the kinds of items you sell, handing them a business card is fast, simple, looks professional, and demonstrates that you take your business seriously.

These days, getting a beautiful set of business cards printed with your shop name, contact details, and even a small image of your work, Etsy avatar, or logo is very quick, easy, and inexpensive.

These handy little cards are a great way to promote your business, and you can include them with your orders or samples of work. Happy customers and supportive friends or family can also help by recommending you to other people. Handing out your business card is an invaluable way to show off your creations beyond your immediate circle.

Design

Here are some tips that you might wish to consider when designing your business cards:

- Keep your card simple, easy to read, and clutter free. Too much text can be a turnoff or just plain confusing.
- Key information to include is: your business name (such as "Sea Glass Jewelry Box"), your personal name or a contact name, your Etsy shop address, as well as an e-mail address.
- Unless you have a dedicated business line, including a phone number is not recommended. A good option is to sign up for Google Voice* (for more information turn to page 88); this will give your customers a contact telephone number that you can control without exposing your direct personal telephone numbers.
- A creative font against a simple background may be plain, but it works, although if it suits your business, choosing a louder color or design may help to make

your card stand out from other business cards. Effects such as embossed text and drop shadows can make the text difficult to read and be distracting.
- If you have a slogan or byline, then you could include it below your logo or business name. This slogan should be something descriptive, catchy, brief, relevant to your shop, and memorable.
- I prefer to stick with standard-size cards (a standard business card size in North America is 2" x 3.5". Unusual shapes and sizes look cool, but I have to admit that when I'm handed cards that don't fit in my wallet they usually end up in a drawer with all those other half-forgotten things!
- Always triple-check your order, making sure all of your contact details are included and are current and correct!

Printing

There are so many great places to get your cards printed, and it helps to ask around for recommendations. Your local stationery store or printer can offer a personal service and helpful opinions, which can be a great comfort if you feel you need a helping hand.

Online printing can be very convenient; you can place your order from the comfort of your home, day or night, and your cards are delivered

*Google Voice is a free service that provides you with a local telephone number that you can set up to automatically forward to any landline of your choice. It can also go directly to voice mail at all times or according to a schedule that you specify. Automatic transcripts of conversations are sent from your Google Voice mail directly to your e-mail box, ensuring that you never miss a message.

to your doorstep. Many sites offer standard templates and layouts, and you can also upload your own design.

If you're going to buy online, it's worth shopping around; read reviews and you can find some surprisingly good deals with reliable companies fiercely competing for your trade. I find that online printing is often cheaper, with bulk orders offering the best value. However, you can also get smaller quantities, which can be a good way to try out a new design or printing company when you're unfamiliar with their service and quality of work.

ACTION STEPS

- ☐ Brainstorm a few logos and designs for your business cards.
- ☐ Create a one-sentence slogan or byline.
- ☐ Sign up for a free Google Voice number.
- ☐ Check standard business card sizes within your country.
- ☐ Ensure all of your details are correct before you submit for printing.

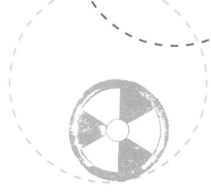

Samples and Promotions

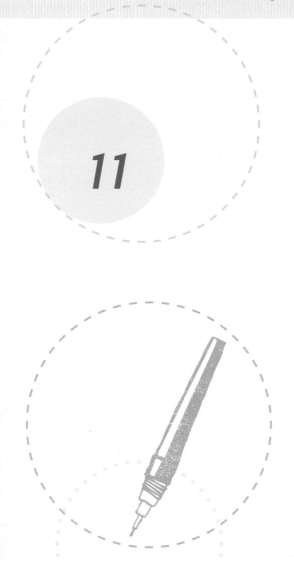

11

I THINK it goes without saying that most people love to receive a little something extra when they place an order: an unadvertised goody or bonus. This can generate goodwill as well as promote your goods, while improving your chances of repeat business and further sales.

The psychologist and author Robert B. Cialdini wrote at length about the law of reciprocity in his wonderful book *Influence: The Psychology of Persuasion*. In short, the law of reciprocity states that people have an inbuilt tendency to return favors; hence the reason you get so many free samples in the mail.

So when someone places an order with you and they receive their item with a further gift hidden in the packing, it can give your shop a boost in their estimation.

Giving away a sample or promotion may only work for certain shops and types of items, but no matter what you're selling, you could include a small voucher with a discount on future items. By making this an unadvertised bonus you still give the recipient an element of surprise and encourage future customers. You could present the voucher in a slightly unusual way, perhaps origami or a nicely designed card, anything that will make it stand out.

Giving away small gifts can have further benefits: they can act as physical reminders of your shop, and if you present them in a fun and creative way people may be more likely to keep them or display them in their homes.

There are many ways of giving away free gifts, but you need to work out what is appropriate for your budget and ensure the gifts tie in with your shop. Ideas include fridge magnets, soaps, creams, lotions, cookies, buttons, small samples of your work, as well as prints.

A great promotional item for artists and photographers is ACEO. If you've never heard of ACEO, the term stands for "Art Cards Editions and Originals." ACEOs are highly collectible, small pieces of artwork, which are a similar size to trading cards. The subject matter for an ACEO can be whatever you like; the only rule is that they measure 2.5"× 3.5".

There are people who collect ACEOs and will search through Etsy just for ACEOs, so by creating ACEOs for sale and as promotional items you can attract a whole new audience.

It's well worth taking a little time to brainstorm ideas for small surprises and gifts that you can send out to your customers, tokens of your appreciation for their custom orders that will encourage a good relationship and increase your chances of future sales.

ACTION STEPS

- ⬭ Create a sample or promotional item to include when you ship your items.
- ⬭ If you sell artwork or photography, then make a variety of ACEOs of your work.

Who Loves You?

12

WHEN YOU'RE selling online, it's always helpful to get feedback on which of your items are the most popular, as well as which are less so, because this gives you a great indication of where to focus your efforts.

If you were selling in a brick-and-mortar store, then you could easily track your items through a simple stock check. You can see which of your items are selling the most on Etsy by visiting "items, sold" but what about people who like your creations but don't buy at the time of viewing? You can click on each listing to see how many "hearts" an item receives, but if you have a full shop this can prove a time-consuming task.

Luckily there's a free online tool, called heart•o•matic, that will tell you in a snapshot exactly how many hearts and favorites your items are receiving:

www.craftcult.com/heartomatic.php

Using heart•o•matic shows you not only how many people have viewed your items but also how many hearts your items have collected and how many people heart/bookmark your shop each day.

From the main page, click on "heart•o•ma-tic" and enter your Etsy username.

You can immediately see how many people have hearted your shop today, as well as on previous days, by clicking on "SHOP HEARTS."

"ITEM HEARTS" gives you a really handy picture of which of your items people are hearting (or bookmarking as favorites). This can indicate the items you may want to focus on making more of and those that are worth taking less time on.

Relisting

When people list a new item on Etsy, it appears on the front page under "Recently Listed Items." This is a fantastic way of gaining a huge amount of exposure with customers who have just opened Etsy in their browser. People who are unsure of what they are shopping for or are just curious may browse through "Recently Listed Items" to find items of interest.

Once your item has been listed, it's not going to appear in "Recently Listed Items" unless you do a "relist," which means your item can appear in this box once again (it's worth noting that there

can be a slight delay between relisting and your item appearing).

Another advantage of relisting is that your items will appear in the top of the results if people run a search within Etsy for items within your niche. For example, if I relisted four of my "sea glass jewelry" items, if someone was searching for "sea glass jewelry" then my items would appear at the top of the search until other people listed new items or ran a relist themselves.

It should be noted that this is an excellent way to gain exposure, but you are charged for it at 20 cents per item. You would also want to relist if your items were about to expire within Etsy's pages (after four months remaining unsold).

To relist (or renew) an item, click on "Your Etsy." You will see a list of your items and above each a little box where you can place a check mark. Select the items that you wish to relist (they must be on the same page). At both the top and bottom of the page, above and below your items, are three options, being "Renew," "Deactivate," and "Delete." Clicking "Renew" will prompt a brief notice confirming that you're about to renew and letting you know how much doing so will cost you. If you agree to the charge, simply click "Renew."

By using "ITEM HEARTS" in heart•o•matic, you can use "reset views" before you make a relist and then see how many new hearts your items receive. This can be a great way of seeing which times of the day your items receive the most views and how effective your relisting campaign was.

Single Items

"SINGLE ITEM HEARTS" does exactly what it says; you can see how many people have hearted one of your items by entering your listing ID. You can also access this information on Etsy by clicking on "See who hearts this item."

"ITEM VIEWS" presents you with a table showing how many views each of your Etsy pages receives, and you can reset this at any time and click "Update" to get the latest information. If you have more than one page of items, you can also see a table that shows how many item views each page of your Etsy shop has received.

"FEATURED" shows you if any of your listings have been shown on the front page of Etsy or on Etsy's blog "The Storque." If you notice that an item suddenly receives a large amount of viewings, this can often be an indication that you have been featured, and you can double-check by using this helpful heart•o•matic resource.

Heart Charts

The heart•o•matic site also includes an exceptionally useful tool that can allow you to have an instant snapshot of your shop's progress, which is called "HEART CHARTS."

"HEART CHARTS" gives you a series of graphs that shows you how many shop hearts you receive per month. This can tell you how many people visit your shop over the year, and you may see increases over the holidays and a tail-off over the summer months, depending on how evergreen your niche is. You can also see the gender of your customers (for those who reveal this data) and how many people are buyers or sellers, among other interesting facts.

You can also see how many item and shop hearts you receive per day, and the final graph, "Heart Activity," shows you the various times of day at which you receive hearts. This is worth taking note of, because if you compare times over sixty days you might spot a trend and this can help you decide when to list new items or make a relist to capitalize on the most viewings.

Pricing

Using heart•o•matic on a daily basis makes tracking your shop's progress easy, and if you spot a spike in hearts but no sales, this could indicate you need to consider your price points. If people are hearting your items but not buying, it doesn't necessarily mean your price is too high, but if items are receiving a lot of hearts and no sales over time, you could test different prices to see if this is a factor.

Some people assume that if they lower their prices they will sell more; it's almost "obvious," and yet it's not always the case. A lot of shoppers associate premium prices with higher value, whether or not that is actually the case, so setting your prices can be a case of experimentation. The heart•o•matic site can be a great aid in deciding how much to charge for your items and which items to focus your attention on, as well as when to list or relist them.

ACTION STEPS

- ☐ Experiment with heart•o•matic and learn the different features on offer.

- ☐ Analyze your hearts—are some items getting hearted more than others?

- ☐ Use heart•o•matic whenever you relist to find the best times of day to list new items and relist older ones.

- ☐ Check your price points—are you receiving lots of hearts but few sales?

- ☐ Set aside ten minutes per day to check your statistics and keep up-to-date with your Etsy shop's progress.

Tracking Your Progress with Google Analytics

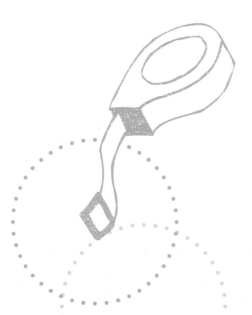

13

AS WELL AS TRACKING your hearts and items through heart•o•matic, it's also extremely useful to understand the metrics of your Etsy shop, especially how many visitors are arriving at your shop on a daily basis.

This knowledge will help you understand how your various promotions, social media, and traffic-generating efforts are paying off. You can also gain an understanding of where your customers are based, which can be vitally important for how you write your listings and the phrases and spellings you use. You can also see how long people are spending on your page and assess whether you need to do more to keep people reading.

All of these options for tracking and understanding your visitors are made possible by using a free piece of software called Google Analytics. I hope by now you've set up your free Google Mail (or Gmail) account (see page 41 for instructions), because this is going to be vital for the next few steps.

Sign in to your Gmail account and then visit:

www.google.com/analytics/

If you're new to Google Analytics you will need to sign up for a new account, which you can do by clicking on "Sign Up Now":

You will then need to enter your Gmail address and password.

On the next page click the "Sign Up" button:

Sign Up for Google Analytics
You are just a few steps from Google Analytics. Click on the **Sign Up** button to get started.

Sign Up »

The next box requires a URL of the Web site you wish to track. Simply add your Etsy shop's URL and give an account name that will help you remember the Web site (in the event that you use Google Analytics to track more than one site).

Then enter your country and time zone before clicking on "Continue."

On the next page, simply enter your last name, first name, and country or territory before clicking "Continue:"

Analytics: New Account Signup
General Information > **Contact Information** > Accept User Agreement > Add Tracking

Last Name:	Sutton
First Name:	Derrick
Country or territory:	United States

The next page requires you to read through Google Analytics' terms and, if in agreement, check the box to say "Yes I agree to the above terms and conditions" and then click on "Create New Account" at the foot of the page.

The following page will give you a code to paste into your Web site to allow tracking. You can ignore this, because you're not a webmaster at Etsy and will not have access to add this code to your shop. So for now, click on "Save and Finish."

On the next page you will find your Google Analytics Tracking Code; this is the information that you will need to copy. To do this, simply highlight the text from "UA-" and the series of digits that follow. For my example below, I will need to highlight and copy "UA-18261496-1":

Website Profiles

Name↑	Reports	Status	Visits
http://www.etsy.com/shop/seaglassjewelrybox UA-5348307-15			

Open another tab in your Web browser, sign in to your Etsy shop, click on "Your Etsy" and then "Shop Settings" and "Options," and select "Web Analytics" from the menu at the top of the page.

You will now see a small box to enter your tracking code, titled "Enter Tracking ID." Simply paste in your Google tracking code and click "Save Changes."

It's worth noting that it can take some time for your tracking code to start working. You may wish to return to this exercise twenty-four hours later to give Google a chance to begin analyzing your site. You will know when your account is active as the yellow ! symbol shown below will become a green check mark:

Statistics

Google Analytics holds an immense amount of information and demographics, far more detail than I can share in this chapter. Therefore, I'm just going to cover the basics, which will allow you to see how your shop and online marketing efforts are progressing.

To access your data, once your account has the green check mark, simply click on "View report":

At the top of your dashboard is a graph, which gives you a snapshot of visits to your shop. This is a helpful feature and something to look for is any sudden spikes in traffic. When you notice spikes in your visits, you will want to investigate further to find out which Web sites have sent you the traffic; perhaps you can contact the Web site owners and offer to write a guest blog or offer mutual linking to your Web site or blog (more on this in a future chapter).

It's also worth noting that you can view this chart by day, week, or month by clicking on the three options in the right-hand corner:

To see which days of the month your visits occurred, simply hold your cursor over the blue points and a pop-up box will tell you which days of the week you're looking at.

As mentioned, I noticed a spike in visitors on August 26, so here is how I can access statistics for this day. First, I click on the drop-down box for the date range at the top of the graph and enter a specific date:

I'll change this to "August 26" and click "Apply" to view that day's traffic:

The first thing you may notice as you change the date is that the "Snapshot" graph has now changed and, instead of showing the days of the month, it now only shows the date you specified:

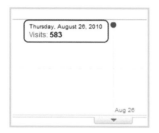

Below this graph is a series of statistics that gives you a wealth of interesting and useful information:

The above statistics tells you how many visits you received that day (when you first sign in to Google Analytics this will default to "Month").

As you can see, on August 26 my Etsy shop received 583 *visits*.

Pageviews shows me that my page received 1,365 views. If a visitor refreshed their browser while on my Etsy shop page, it will count as another view. Similarly, if someone clicks on the second page of my Etsy listings and then clicks back, this will also count as another view. This explains why there were almost double the Pageviews in relation to unique visitors.

Pages/Visit shows me that an average of 2.34 of my Etsy shop's pages were visited. Depending on the amount of items you have listed, you may only have a few pages, so bear this in mind when you use this statistic.

Bounce Rate shows me the percentage of people who visited my shop and then immediately clicked off to another page or Web site or hit the "back button." Seventy percent is high and might indicate that the source of this sudden spike in traffic is perhaps not fully related to my

Etsy shop and there could be a number of reasons for this high figure. Overall, when I look at my shop over the course of a month, the bounce rate is much lower at 54 percent, which means more people stay on my shop and browse through my items. Essentially, the lower the bounce rate the better!

Avg. Time on Site gives you the average amount of time your visitors spend in your Etsy shop. You will want to see this figure increase. I hope after you have optimized your listings and shop using the lessons in this book you will encourage visitors to read through your listings and spend more time browsing in your Etsy shop. If this number is low, then it gives you a good indication that you need to work on your shop and in engaging and entertaining your visitors.

New Visits tells you how many of the people coming to your Etsy shop are brand-new, rather than returning customers and shoppers.

Below "Site Usage" is a small box giving you a snapshot of your visitors. This is exactly the same as the main graphic that shows when you first click on "View report":

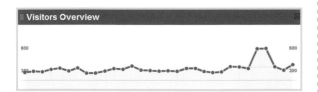

To the right-hand side of "Visitors Overview" is the "Content Overview" box, which gives you a brief overview of the top five pages within your Etsy shop or Web site to which you have the most visitors.

Below your Content Overview is "Map Overlay":

The details contained within "Map Overlay" are, again, highly useful. By clicking on any of the countries shown on the map you can see more detail. For this example, I'll click on the map of the United States.

The darker the color, the more visitors. From below, I can see the majority of my visitors are from California. Using this information, I could look into related Web sites or blogs based in California and see if any of these accept advertising. This is just one way I could use this information, and as you become more proficient in Internet marketing you will find more and more possibilities.

When you click on a state, you get additional information below the map:

You can then click on each city for even more detail.

Going back to the map of the world, you can get a good idea of how many people are visiting you from other countries. If you notice a high amount of visitors in Great Britain and Australia, for example, you will definitely want to make sure you are using their spellings for your listings, for instance, using "jewellery" as well as "jewelry."

Traffic Sources

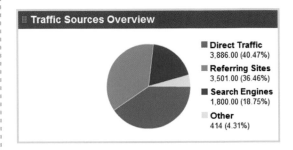

The "Traffic Sources" box shows you a pie chart of where your Etsy traffic is coming from. As you can see, *direct traffic* is the larger proportion, with over 40 percent of traffic coming from Etsy.

I have a high amount of *referring sites* also, at 36.46 percent, which reflects the amount of social media and Web 2.0 techniques I use (and will explain later in the book). When you first start out, your direct traffic will be the highest percentage, but as you begin to promote yourself online these numbers will change.

The *search engines* sent me 18.75 percent of visitors, and *"Other"* is non-organic and non-direct traffic.

Spikes

Going back to the spike in traffic that I received on August 26, I would click on Traffic Sources' "view report" for further information:

Top Traffic Sources

Sources	Visits	% visits
(direct) ((none))	253	43.40%
epbot.com (referral)	77	13.21%
google (organic)	67	11.49%
facebook.com (referral)	22	3.77%

Using "Top Traffic Sources," I can see that a spike in my visitors came from a Web site called epbot.com, which would definitely be worth further investigation to see why visitors came to my shop. Perhaps there will be an opportunity to engage further with this Web site.

It's always immensely helpful to know exactly where your traffic is coming from and how your online marketing campaigns are paying off, as well as where you can find further opportunities and focus your attentions.

Exclude Yourself!

Something to watch for, which can really throw your stats, is your IP address. Because you'll be spending a large amount of time within your Etsy shop, your Google Analytics statistics for bounce rate and time spent on site will be influenced by your own visits and this will affect the data. For this reason, you will need to exclude your IP address.

First, you will need to take note of your IP address. If you're unsure of your address visit:

www.whatismyip.com/

At the top of the page will be a series of numbers, which indicate your IP address.

Now go back to your main Google Analytics page by clicking on the "Google Analytics" logo at the top of the page.

From here you will need to click on "Edit" from the right-hand side of your account details:

On the next page, scroll down towards the bottom to "Filters Applied to Profile":

Then click "Add Filter":

Now enter your IP address in the "Filter Name" box and use the following settings:

Select "Add **new** filter for Profile"

Filter Name: My IP Address (this is a note to yourself, so write anything that will remind you are blocking your own IP address from Google Analytics)

Check "Predefined Filter"

Enter the following options from the next dropdown menu: "Exclude," "traffic from the IP Addresses," "that are equal to."

IP Address—enter your IP Address, which you got from www.whatismyip.com in the earlier step.

Then click "Save Changes" and you're finished!

As mentioned earlier, Google Analytics is a complex and detailed resource and the amount of information it carries can be incredibly useful, but for newcomers it can also be a little overwhelming.

I would suggest using YouTube or a similar free online video resource to search for further lessons on Google Analytics and gradually build up your pool of knowledge over time. You can also find a ton of great tips concerning Google Analytics and Etsy within the Etsy forums.

For now, though, you can easily see how much traffic your shop is receiving and where your visitors are coming from, and you can begin to use this data to streamline your listings and efforts.

ACTION STEPS

- Sign up for a Google Analytics account through your Etsy shop's Gmail account.
- Add your tracking ID into Etsy Web Analytics, linking your Etsy shop and Google Analytics account.
- Familiarize yourself with the basics of the Google Analytics statistics.
- Return after a week has passed (allowing Google Analytics to gather data from your Etsy shop) and note locations of visitors and the Web sites that send you traffic.
- Check your Google Analytics at least once a week; pay attention to "spikes" and any weak areas where you can improve your statistics through optimizing your Etsy shop.
- *Optional step*: search on YouTube and the Etsy forums for additional lessons in Google Analytics, tips, and techniques.

Connecting on the Etsy Forums

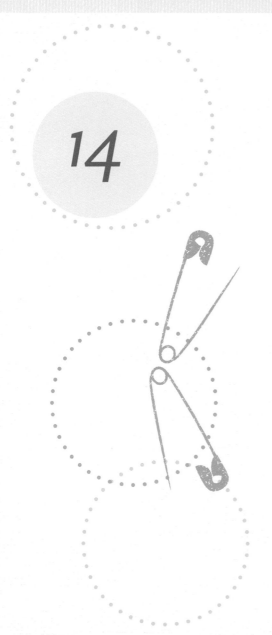

14

THE ETSY forums are not only a helpful place to find a wealth of advice and useful information; they're also an excellent place to promote your shop, as well as connect with fellow Etsy sellers and buyers.

To access the Etsy forums, visit your Etsy shop and click on "Community":

On the next page, click on "Forums":

One of the best ways to build a solid presence on Etsy is by becoming an active member within the forums. Not only can you potentially bring new traffic to your shop, but you can also provide and receive help from other Etsy members. Many of the chapters within this book concern social networking, and a recurring theme is helping others and giving real value, which in turn can lead others to helping you.

Whenever you post on the Etsy forums or blogs and Web sites, you should take care to offer positive and constructive comments. A lot of people miss the fact that posting material online creates a "digital footprint" (if you use the same username to post with) and this can be a great help in building your online presence in a positive and helpful light.

Occasionally, you find people on the forums who are blatantly spamming; this is a short-term tactic and rarely brings rewards, so take care not to constantly push people to your items or shop. The best way to get people to visit your shop is by giving helpful advice and tips or thought-provoking comments. People's natural sense of curiosity will often lead them to click on your avatar to see what you're selling.

If time is limited, you could set aside fifteen minutes of each day to look through some of the questions and topics in the forums and see if there are any ways you can contribute. Over time you'll see the same questions coming up and you will be able to answer them in no time at all.

There are a number of different categories to which you can post questions and answers and it's worth browsing through each of them.

Site Help

If you have experience with selling on Etsy, a great place to start is with the "Site Help" category. Even if you've only been selling for a short while, you may still be able to answer questions. While glancing through these questions and answers, you will find new solutions from fellow sellers. Not only can this be helpful for your development on Etsy, but you'll also be able to answer these questions if they're asked in the future.

It can be helpful to find topics that have fewer than ten comments, which means your response will stay on the first page for the topic. Commenting on topics running to multiple pages is still helpful and a good way to contribute, but you're less likely to be noticed and your post can get lost, although if the subject matter is of interest, participating can be rewarding in itself.

It's often said that you find out how much you've learned as you teach others, so any participation on the forums can help build your Etsy knowledge base.

Business Topics

You can pick up a lot of helpful information in the "Business Topics" category. You will also find people asking for advice and you may be able to offer solutions. If *you* have a question, then posting a new topic is a great way to find answers and you may also get to know fellow sellers.

One of the posts that stood out as an excellent example of engaging people and drawing attention to one's shop at the same time concerned a lady who asked for constructive critiques of her avatar. Whether or not this was calculated, it really helped bring her attention, as the threads soon ran to pages of responses, with the majority of contributors clicking on the poster's avatar and visiting her shop. People were checking out the lady's avatar to see if it tied in with her banner and, in doing so, were glancing through her items. I'd imagine if she checked her shop in heart•o•matic, she'd have seen her viewings and hearts increasing and, on the back of this, her sales.

Promotions

The "Promotions" category is perfect if you're considering running a campaign to increase traffic to your shop. Before trying out a new promotion on this part of the forum, I recommend you have a look through some of the promotion topics currently running. You can see by the amount of replies and posts how successful these threads are. It's also worth looking at the shops that are running their promotions. For instance, I just spotted a post that has over one thousand responses and is giving away $30 in shop credit for

people to post a comment and be entered into a raffle. While this is a large number of responses, the shop's sales appear to have increased but not significantly. So was this promotional campaign worth the $30 credit?

Promotions work and can raise awareness for Etsy sellers, but if you're going to take part in a giveaway or competition it's worth doing some research and factoring in the cost of materials and the time spent creating your items.

There are a variety of ways to use the Etsy forums, and becoming active can help to raise awareness for your shop and give you new ideas and tips for your own creations, as well as helping others to improve their Etsy experience.

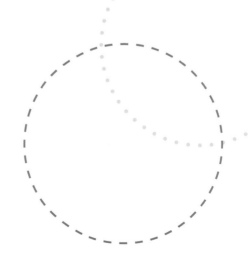

ACTION STEPS

- Familiarize yourself with the various categories in the forums.

- Search for questions to which you can provide answers.

- Look for posts with ten comments or fewer for maximum exposure (although it's always a good idea to contribute).

- Add value whenever you post.

- Create a post for the "Promotions" category.

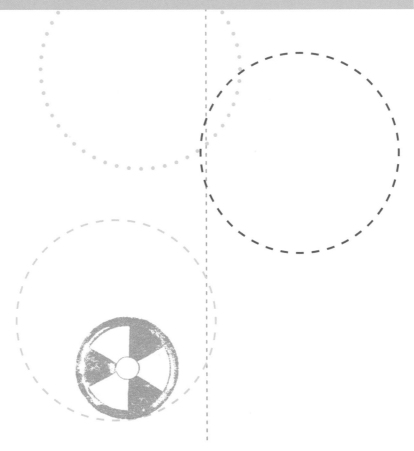

Joining and Forming Etsy Teams

15

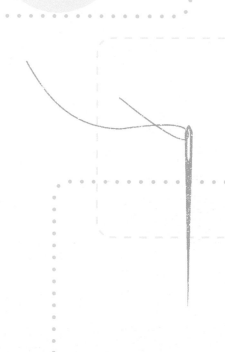

JOINING or forming an Etsy team can have similar benefits to taking part in the Etsy forums. By becoming a part of an Etsy team, you can find new ways to network and share information with fellow artists and crafters and make new friends and contacts with other creative people within your location or niche. Often Etsy teams will have meet-ups, especially if you look for a local team in your nearest city.

Sellers as Buyers

One reason for meeting and chatting with fellow sellers is that two heads are better than one. Interacting with other sellers can help you to promote your shop, as well as help other people with their shops.

You'll often find that Etsy sellers are also Etsy buyers, which is another great reason to network and connect with fellow Etsyians. Both I and my wife have sold on Etsy, and at least half of the gifts we buy for friends and family for birthdays and the holidays are from other Etsy shops. Buying from fellow Etsy team members is an excellent way to support fellow crafters and artists, and you may find you start to make some sales, too.

Critiques

In chapter 14, I mentioned asking for critiques of your shop in the Etsy forums as a great way to get feedback and visitors to your shop, and you can really learn a lot by asking some frank questions. If you ask for a critique of your shop from a fellow team member you may get a far more specific "review." A fellow team member may be able to suggest ways you can improve your tags or listings because they are in the same niche as you. They may also be able to suggest marketing strategies that you might not have considered.

Promotion

Another advantage to joining an Etsy team is that members often promote one another's products, which, depending on the size of the team, can be hugely beneficial. Some Etsy teams also group together to "bulk buy," cutting the costs of otherwise expensive materials.

You can also cross-promote fellow team members' shops by including fellow sellers on your Facebook Page or tweeting about their latest items. While promoting another seller may seem strange, it can increase your visitors and sales when they promote you in return, as you will also reach their Twitter followers or Facebook fans. I wouldn't recommend this if you're vying for the same market as another seller, but often you will find other artists or crafters are selling completely different items than you.

ACTION STEPS

- ◻ Join or form an Etsy team.
- ◻ Contribute to your team by helping others and providing constructive criticism or guidance.
- ◻ If you create a new team, search for sellers within your niche whom you can invite to join by posting within the Etsy forums.

Creating Etsy Treasuries

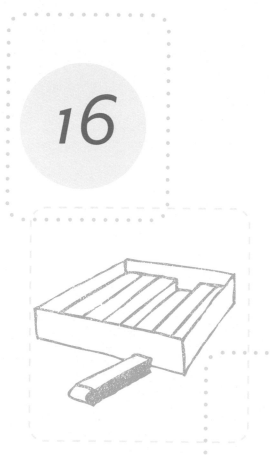

16

AN ETSY Treasury is a gallery of various sellers' items that has been created by an Etsy member. It is often a grouping of favorite items, usually centered around a theme.

To get a good idea of how treasuries work, visit:

www.etsy.com/treasury/

There are so many ways to promote your shop within Etsy, and the technique covered in this chapter can be a lot of fun! This could be viewed as a slightly strange strategy because it focuses on featuring other people's work. While this concept may sound unusual, bear with me!

By featuring other people in your "treasury," you bring at least eleven (if you choose to feature one of your items as well) people to your shop. If you make your treasury eye-catching and appealing, it might even appear on Etsy's front page. As soon as one of your items appears on the front page, you'll often experience a huge spike in viewings and, I hope, sales.

Etsy mentions in their treasury guide that if you feature yourself in a treasury and it gets promoted to their front page, then your item might not be included. This is because treasuries aren't designed for self-promotion, and this is definitely something to bear in mind when you create your treasury. You will notice a recurring theme throughout this book, which is always to avoid hammering people with your sales message. Because it's a good idea to avoid continuous self-promotion, creating a treasury can be a subtle way to bring people to your Etsy shop while entertaining your audience and connecting with fellow artists and crafters.

Making a Treasury

Before you make a treasury, it's worth reading up on Etsy's guidelines to ensure you increase your chances of it being accepted and promoted.

One of the first considerations for building your treasury is your "theme." Themes can be anything from colors (which are common strands in treasuries), to movies, comics, nature, cities, and animals—pretty much anything you can think of! For my running example of sea glass jewelry, I would make a treasury based on the beach or the sea.

It's a good idea to keep a sense of consistency, vivid images, or eye-catching colors as well as a varied range of prices. It's also a good idea to check the sellers you'll be featuring and make sure they have good feedback.

You will need to choose twelve items for your

treasury, plus four to act as alternatives in case featured items sell before the treasury is live. Once you have your theme worked out, try searching for sellers' items to feature by typing in your keyword into the Etsy search bar:

As you find an item, you could either bookmark it in your browser or add it to your Etsy favorite sellers so you have a record to refer back to.

When you're ready to create your treasury, visit:

www.etsy.com/treasury/

Then click on "Create a List" on the right-hand side of the page.

Next you need to add a title for your treasury, as well as a description. Try to create an interesting and compelling title, something that will intrigue people to click on your treasury above the others that are featured.

You can also change your privacy settings if you want to keep your treasury private, but for the purposes of this exercise you would want this setting to be on the default setting, which allows everyone to view this list. Below there is also an option to include some tags to help people find your treasury, so for my example I might include "beach," "sea glass", "ocean," et cetera.

You will need to enter the URLs of the twelve

items that will make up your treasury (as well as the four alternatives) and click "Save."

Once your treasury is live on Etsy, it's a good idea to send a quick message to each of the people you've featured. This is common courtesy and also a great way to get to know other Etsy sellers. There is also a chance that they may visit your shop and potentially refer you to other people.

An additional chance for exposure comes from the possibility that these twelve (or eleven if you feature one of your items) sellers may e-mail a link of your treasury to their friends and family, which could bring even more people to your shop.

Making treasuries is a wonderful way to engage on Etsy, to meet new people and raise the possibilities that you will be included in other people's treasuries. It's also a fun way of inadvertently promoting yourself while taking part in a creative pursuit; finding colors or items that match a theme requires creativity, and it's as though you're embarking on your own treasure hunt. Coming up with great titles for your treasuries also gives you good practice for creating catchy and compelling slogans, which is an invaluable set of skills when it comes to marketing.

If you make enough treasuries, which people can really connect with and enjoy, people on Etsy may get to know your name, which is always helpful. The more opportunities you get to interact with other Etsy sellers, the more you become a part of this often supportive and inspiring community.

ACTION STEPS

- ☐ Browse through existing Etsy Treasuries to see how they are constructed and to get a feel for themes.
- ☐ Brainstorm and note down a series of ideas for your own Etsy Treasury.
- ☐ Choose sixteen items to include in your Etsy Treasury.
- ☐ Find a free slot for your new treasury.
- ☐ Contact the sellers you included and let them know they've been featured.

Get Ahead in the Holidays

17

THE HOLIDAYS are an ideal time to promote your shop on Etsy; it's also a very competitive time, with sellers vying for eager shoppers.

One tactic for capitalizing on the holidays is by making sure you have a good plan in place. Anticipating the upcoming holidays months ahead can give you the jump on your competition. If you use Google Mail for your Etsy shop, as recommended, then you can set up Google Calendar to prompt you; indeed, any other form of calendar can help.

Planning

Many retail stores place orders and plan for holidays months ahead. I'm sure you've noticed this, Easter being promoted just as Christmas ends! Of course you don't need to follow this extreme, but thinking ahead is a good idea.

By placing orders for materials months ahead, you can avoid vying with other sellers who may be frantically trying to acquire the same materials on eBay and from suppliers. This could drive your costs down on bids and help to ensure items are in stock when you need them.

You can also attract a whole new audience of shoppers by including the holidays in your tags, but be sure you avoid tagging your items with "Christmas," "Easter," "Halloween," et cetera, if your items are not specifically tailored to these holidays.

Using incorrect tags is against Etsy's terms, and you may be asked to remove or rename your tags and remove offending items. Mistagging also causes problems for customers. If you're looking for a specific item and you find a shop via a tag and it's not selling the item you're looking for, it can be frustrating and you might be unlikely to consider buying from the shop in the future.

If you have items that are designed for specific holidays, then using the relevant tags could improve traffic to your Etsy shop.

You could also produce a small catalog showcasing some of your best holiday-themed items and include this when you pack and ship orders. By using a holiday theme for your catalog you could associate your Etsy shop with the upcoming holiday in the buyer's mind.

Confidence

Another way to improve your holiday sales is instilling confidence in anxious buyers by changing your shop announcement for the holidays. For instance, perhaps you could write a seasonal-based announcement through November and December that will let people know you can deliver over the holiday season.

When people are shopping for the holidays, they can often be in "panic mode." If you have a well-written announcement that states you ship within twenty-four hours of payment and are happy to include priority mail (providing they pay), you may appeal to anxious shoppers and thereby increase your sales.

Shop Policies

You can also answer any last-minute shopping concerns by making sure you fill out your "Shop Policies." You can access these by visiting "Your Etsy," "Shop Setting," "Info & Appearance"; then select "Policies" from the menu at the top of the page.

Areas to include are:

- Payment: it's a good idea to request immediate payment if you want to be able to ship quickly, and you can also let people know that if they wish to make any other arrangements, then they are free to contact you.
- Shipping: State the types of shipping you use for items, whether it's first class, which carrier you use, and if you provide

discounts for more than one item. You should also reiterate how quickly you dispatch. For international orders, you will need to fill out a customs slip and you may wish to make a note that customs charges are out of your jurisdiction.

- Refunds and Exchanges: What are your policies regarding exchanges or damaged items? It's worth considering these points and including them here.
- Additional Policies and FAQs: this is a great place to include important details, such as letting people know the best way to contact and reach you.

When it comes to your general and shipping policies, you should try to ensure you create a sense of prompt and friendly service. It can be a good exercise to put yourself in the shoes of the person shopping for a last-minute holiday or anniversary gift; they're going to want someone reliable and personable, someone who can alleviate their anxiety and deliver on time.

ACTION STEPS

- Make a note of upcoming holidays in your calendar or task manager for early notification.
- Buy materials ahead of time.
- Change your shop announcement for the holidays (and remember to change it back to its original announcement afterwards).
- Check your shipping policy and ensure it gives last-minute customers confidence that they will receive items in time for the holidays or other special occasions.

Your Google Places

18

GOOGLE PLACES is a free resource that gets millions of searches each day and can be a fantastic way of getting your Etsy shop some more exposure.

After including her Etsy shop on Google Places, my wife made some local sales to places literally within a five-mile radius. For a few moments' work, you can add your shop and potentially make some local sales.

People are increasingly turning to shopping locally. With environmental concerns close to a lot of people's hearts, it's good to know that you can buy products that won't contribute to a huge carbon footprint. Another benefit is the knowledge that you're supporting local artists and crafters; plus you receive your items quicker!

With Google Places you can list your working hours, include a Google Map of your location (which is perfect if you have an open studio or brick-and-mortar shop), and also include photographs of your items, as well as coupons if you decide to try local promotions.

Privacy

One thing worth noting is that submitting your home address and personal phone number may be less than ideal for many people. Two ways around this are to use a PO box address and Google Voice.

Google Voice allows you to have one phone number to which you can direct all calls. For instance, you can have calls coming through to your home phone or cell phone. For Google Places, you could provide people with your Google Voice number and set it to only call between the hours that suit you. This way you also keep your cell or home number private.

To find out more about Google Voice, visit:

www.google.com/googlevoice/about.html

Once you're ready to add your Etsy shop to Google Places, go to:

www.google.com/local/add/businessCenter

On the right-hand side of the page, click on "List your business" and then fill out your Etsy shop name and the additional information that Google asks for.

In the Web site address field you can add your Etsy shop, Gmail address, and, where it asks for a description, a short advertisement for your shop. Once you fill in the category most relevant for your Etsy shop (adding further categories where relevant), click "Next."

Opening Hours

The Basic Information section requires a category for your business and also your "Shop hours," and you can either add your shop hours or "prefer not to specify," whichever is best for you.

Payment

For your payment options, you can include a variety of different choices, but the main method of payment for Etsy shops is PayPal, so this is probably the best option for this field.

Pictures

Google Places allows you to upload up to ten pictures from your computer. You should take some time to select your very best images, and this is vital because you want to hook local searchers. Something to consider is that you won't just be competing with other Etsy shops; potentially, you'll be competing with brick-and-mortar stores as well. Your competition will be anyone in your local area who wishes to appear in Google Places within the same niche as you.

For this exercise, I would create a special folder on my computer and name it "Google Places." Then I would go through my photographs and copy and paste the very best into this folder. This saves me having to search through hundreds of photographs when it comes to upload. I recommend the same technique throughout the book wherever you need to upload content, because it helps to keep things organized and simple.

Another option with uploading pictures is to provide a Web address, so technically you could paste in the URLs of your ten best Etsy items but I wouldn't recommend this in case the URL changes or the item sells.

Videos

You will also get the opportunity to add videos from YouTube. Unless you have already made YouTube videos of your creations, you may wish to come back to this step after you've read the YouTube chapter, which will take you through the process of making your own promotional videos.

Once you're finished on this page, click "Submit" and you're done.

Depending on whether or not this is your first visit, you will have two options to verify your account, by phone or by mail. The mail option can take up to two weeks; therefore, I recommend the phone option so that you can be up and running as soon as possible. Either way, you'll receive a PIN, which you will need to enter to verify your account.

When you log in to Google Places, your "Business Info" on the right-hand side of the page shows your status. Once you return after reading the YouTube chapter and add your video URL, your status should read: "100% complete." If you have missed adding anything, you can always click on "Edit" and add more information at any point.

It can sometimes take up to twenty-four hours for Google to make changes, so please allow for this.

Once your account is verified and live, you can check your Google Places listing by visiting Google Maps and typing in your shop name. Hopefully your shop will be showing, which may lead to local sales as well as introducing local searchers to your Etsy shop.

ACTION STEPS

- Set up a Google Voice number (if you haven't already).
- Add your Etsy shop to Google Places.
- Make a note to return and add your own YouTube video once you have created it (which you will learn how to do in Chapter 32).

Submitting to dmoz

19

Dmoz

A LITTLE-KNOWN WEB SITE (at least outside of the Internet marketing community) is dmoz, which is the "Open Directory Project," comprising a huge directory of Web sites that are edited and maintained by a global community of volunteers, just like Wikipedia.

Getting your Etsy shop listed on dmoz has two benefits: first, people searching dmoz may find your listing; and second, you receive a powerful backlink for your Etsy shop.

So what is a backlink? Web sites gain authority through the relevance and quality of content on their pages and also through links that point to them from other sites. Links that point from other sites to yours are known as backlinks.

Not all backlinks are equal; you can get a backlink from lots of places, but if the Web sites linking to you have a low page rank, then these are worth less than a site with a high page rank.

Etsy, for instance, has a page rank of 7/10, which is powerful, and Google has a page rank of

10/10. Dmoz has a page rank of 8/10, so receiving a backlink from dmoz can be a real boost to your blog and Etsy shop.

Page Rank

If you ever wish to see the page rank of a Web site, you can download a free add-on for Mozilla Firefox called Search Status by visiting:

addons.mozilla.org/en-US/firefox/addon/321/

If you enter a search for "Search Status add-on" in YouTube, you will find plenty of simple tutorials that will show you how to use this Firefox add-on.

This is an important lesson, because some people believe that if they get a backlink from a Web site it will boost their own Web site's ranking. This is partially true (any backlink is a bonus!), but not all backlinks are equal.

If you're investing time into building backlinks by searching on blogs and Web sites within your niche that allow comments or maybe accept a backlink exchange (you link to them on your blog, they link to you), then it's good to know their page rank in advance. However, it should also be noted that while you will definitely benefit from high-page-rank backlinks, you should also have a natural spread of backlinks, including page-rank-zero sites. Any signs of trying to "game the system" could have negative effects for your ranking, so maintaining a balance to your backlinking strategy is vital. If you find an interesting article on a Web site that relates to your niche, then leaving a comment with your URL is going to be beneficial no matter what the Web site's page rank is.

Going back to dmoz, because the site has such a high page rank, this quick and simple exercise is a worthwhile investment of your time. To submit your Etsy shop to dmoz, visit:

www.dmoz.org/

The first page shows you various categories, and you need to choose one that will be a fit for your shop. For my sample sea glass jewelry shop, I'll choose "Shopping" from the front page. On the next page, "Jewelry" would be my next choice, and on the following page, as there are no obvious fits for sea glass, I'll select "Handcrafted," and on the next page "Glass," which is the closest match.

It's really important that you choose the best option for the items you're selling, because your submission will be monitored by a human (rather than automated script) and if you post to the wrong category they may reject your application.

Once you've drilled down to the best category for your Etsy shop, click on "suggest URL" in the menu at the very top of the dmoz Web site.

You will now be taken to a page to submit further details. There is a link to the guidelines, which are worth reading to ensure you have the best chance of being accepted, and a big yellow bar that shows you an example of how to submit.

If you're uncertain where to post or open a new tab or browser window, head to the dmoz home page and run a search using a keyword for the type of items you sell. If other shops or Web sites are listed, this should bring up some examples, and you can always visit these Web sites as a fail-safe way of checking this is the correct category for you.

The category will be filled in for you when you click "suggest URL." Below this box is a place to post your Etsy shop's URL. I recommend visiting your Etsy shop, clicking on the "Shop Home" option, and then copying and pasting the URL, to avoid errors.

The next box asks for "Title of Site," with a blurb below explaining how to fill this out. You should use your shop name; my example would be "Sea Glass Jewelry." This should be typed naturally; don't use all CAPS and also avoid being promotional, i.e., "Fantastic, affordable, unique Sea Glass Jewelry"!

The box below requests a description of your site and gives further recommendations, which are essential to read through and follow. Once you've filled in your description you could copy your text and paste it into a spell-checker, either online or in a word-processing document to double-check spelling and grammar.

You then need to enter your e-mail address, a "User Verification" or "Captcha" (a random series of letters and numbers), read through the Submission Agreement, and confirm you understand the guidelines before clicking "Submit."

The dmoz site is staffed by volunteers, so if your submission is accepted, it may take some time to show, and this can take weeks or even months.

Once you've submitted your shop, it's best to try to put it out of your mind and move on. You've just taken a quick step to give your shop a boost with the search engines and you can repeat this exercise with your blog (more on blogs later in Chapter 25) or Web site and any other shops you own.

Registering with the Search Engines

While you're registering with dmoz, it makes sense to submit your site to the three big search engines at the same time: Bing, Google, and Yahoo! This is a short exercise and a real "set and forget," which may bring benefits to your shop, blog, and Web site further down the line.

Although Google is considered the number one search engine, there are still a lot of people who use Bing (formerly MSN Search) and Yahoo! so you want to cover all bases.

Before you submit, it's a good idea to double-check and see if you're already registered. To do this simply visit Bing, Google, and Yahoo! and type in your Etsy shop name. If your shop shows in the results, you do not need to take any further action.

If your site is not showing, here are the links to submit your sites to:

bing.com/webmaster/SubmitSitePage.aspx

google.com/addurl/

siteexplorer.search.yahoo.com/

ACTION STEPS

- ☐ Add Search Status to your Mozilla Firefox browser.
- ☐ Submit your Etsy shop to dmoz.
- ☐ Add any additional sites you may own to dmoz.
- ☐ Check that your Etsy shop is listed with Bing, Google, and Yahoo! and, if not, submit to each using the links provided in this chapter.

Stumbling with StumbleUpon

20

STUMBLEUPON is a wonderful place to market your Etsy shop and also have some fun! You can enter a phrase on virtually any topic and make a "Stumble," which will come back with a huge variety of related Web sites. Within a short time you can find yourself in all sorts of corners of the Internet, many of which you may never have known existed.

StumbleUpon has a very large community of users (at the time of writing, over 9 million) who provide links to sites and Web pages they've discovered, rating videos, Web sites, photography, shopping results, and a huge wealth of other information.

StumbleUpon is well worth investigating for sheer browsing entertainment alone, but the reason we'll be using it in this book is for further promotion of our Etsy shops.

You can use the StumbleUpon toolbar with Internet Explorer, Google Chrome, or Mozilla Firefox, which I am going to use for this example.

You can download Firefox by visiting:

www.mozilla.com/firefox/

Once you've installed and run Firefox, visit the link below and click "Install":

addons.mozilla.org/en-US/firefox/addon/138

Toolbars sometimes get bad press for slowing down browsers, but I've used StumbleUpon for a couple of years now and never had an issue.

As soon as you've installed the StumbleUpon toolbar, restart Firefox, and it should now appear as a new toolbar within your browser.

The main function of the StumbleUpon toolbar that you'll be using is the thumbs-up symbol, which is next to the Stumble! logo.

For a trial, go to your Etsy shop, choose one of your items, and click on it so that your listing is showing. Then go to the StumbleUpon toolbar and click the thumbs-up "I like it."

Review

The box may default to the "Quick Submit" feature, but I recommend you select the "Add a review" tab, as this will give you more options.

The first option asks "Is this site safe for work?" (Click "Yes" if applicable.) Choosing "safe for work" can increase your audience, although if you're selling items with an adult theme on Etsy, then you need to announce it on the "safe for

work?" option to avoid any issues with your StumbleUpon account.

Next select a topic; if I were Stumbling a piece of sea glass jewelry then I would select "Shopping." You will also need to add tags, and you could use five relevant tags from your Etsy listings.

When you write a review for a product, you should aim to keep it both brief and enticing. For instance:

> A treasure from the sea!
> A wonderful necklace made with some beautiful sea glass jewels!

Once you've chosen your topic, filled in the tags, left a review, and chosen "Language" (it's English by default), click "Add Review" and you're done!

It can be interesting to make a note of your item views prior to Stumbling and then see how they increase post-StumbleUpon.

Responsible Social Bookmarking

While you should definitely Stumble some of your own Etsy items, you should also visit other Web sites and pages and Stumble them, too. This is a common theme in the book and a technique I recommend for all forms of "social bookmarking." If you only bookmark your items and Web sites, then you can quickly be seen as a spammer and this could cause your account to be suspended.

The best way to view StumbleUpon is, as with any other community, as a place to get to know people and share conversations and compliments. For example, it's unlikely you would approach someone at a party that you'd never met and say, "Hi, I just made a really nice necklace. Do you want to buy it?" But if you got to know someone through chatting about shared interests, then they might be more predisposed to buy your jewelry—providing that they were in the shopping mood. Similarly, if you engage people by providing them with links and recommendations on a wide variety of topics that they find of interest and *then* promote yourself occasionally, your audience is more inclined to see you as a contributor adding to the community, rather than someone who is merely using it for self-promotional purposes.

If you already have a presence on Twitter or Facebook, then you may have seen people who send out endless sales messages. I don't know about you, but personally I "unfollow" them very quickly!

On the other hand, when people send me links to interesting topics and humorous Web sites I look forward to their tweets (or Stumbles) and when they drop in the occasional sales message I'm far more disposed to read it.

Su.pr

StumbleUpon also has a fantastic service that you can use to shorten URLs and post to Twitter and Facebook with one click. Twitter is covered in far more detail in Chapter 24, but for now please bookmark or make a note of this site:

su.pr/

Su.pr is a StumbleUpon service designed to shorten URLs. When you find a Web site you'd like to share, its Web address (or URL) can be quite long and you may wish to shorten it. You can also track the amount of visits and clicks your link generates.

For instance, here's the URL for my imaginary Etsy shop:

etsy.com/shop/SeaglassJewelryBoxExample

This is 40 characters and when you post to Twitter you're limited to 140 characters, so you've already used 40 before you've had a chance to write anything. Su.pr will help you to shorten this so you can write more in your tweet.

Here's how you can use Su.pr to shorten a URL. First, copy and paste the link you wish to share and rather than click "Post," use the "Just Shorten" button. This will give you an abbreviated URL, which will have a Web address of http://su.pr/ followed by a few digits.

By shortening your URLs, you have more

characters to use. If I was posting to Twitter, by having more space free I would have more chances of adding text that would, I hope, compel people to click on my link.

If you're signed in to Su.pr you also have an option to post to Twitter and Facebook, which can save you a lot of time.

You can also post directly to StumbleUpon and they provide you with additional information, including how many people have clicked on your link, how many times it's been retweeted (more on retweeting later), and which time of the day your links get the most viewings.

This is essential data that allows you to see how popular and effective your social-bookmarking efforts have been.

That's the power of the Internet and how you can go from an Etsy shop with very little traffic and sales to a successful shop with plenty of viewings. With the wealth of free tools available online, you don't need to spend hours in your promotional efforts; indeed, social bookmarking can be a quick and fun job.

I recommend using both Su.pr and the StumbleUpon toolbar as the occasion demands. I use Su.pr when I wish to post to Facebook, StumbleUpon, and Twitter with one click and the StumbleUpon toolbar for when I want to share a quick link or news story within my niche.

Because you will need to ensure you're bookmarking plenty of links (other than your own), I recommend using the StumbleUpon toolbar for this purpose and using Su.pr when you're sending out more targeted Stumbles (and tweets) to your followers on StumbleUpon, Twitter, and Facebook.

There are plenty of online tools detailed in this book, and becoming proficient in each of them is a good idea so that you can find the simplest way to broadcast to your audience.

ACTION STEPS

- Install the StumbleUpon toolbar in your Web browser.
- Give one of your items a Stumble using StumbleUpon.
- Search through StumbleUpon and give news stories and fellow artists or creators a thumbs-up.
- Bookmark Su.pr and use it to share links.

Flickr—Your Online Photo Album

21

FLICKR is a Web site owned by Yahoo! and allows you to post and share your photographs online. There are many reasons to use Flickr, one being that if you want to share photographs with friends and family, then having them all in one folder, which everyone can access, is much easier than e-mailing photographs to people separately.

Flickr is a safe environment to share your photographs because you can make your account private so that only people you trust have access; however, for the purpose of this chapter and marketing of your Etsy creations, you will want to make your Flickr account public.

Please note that if you already have a Flickr account, which you are using for personal reasons, it might be easier to sign up for a new Yahoo! e-mail account (using your Etsy shop name) and a fresh Flickr account to use for your Etsy shop.

To get started on Flickr you'll need to create a Yahoo! ID, which you can get here:

login.yahoo.com/

You then need to visit Flickr to open a new account:

www.flickr.com/

On the right-hand of the page you will see "Create Your Account." Click here to enter your new Yahoo! e-mail address.

Name

After you've entered some fairly typical details, you'll be prompted to "choose your new Flickr screen name."

Where possible use your Etsy shop name or, if this has been taken, try to make a slight adjustment; for instance, if "sea glass jewelry" was taken, you could try "sea glass jewelry shop" or "sea glass jewelry box."

The next screen invites you to personalize your Flickr account:

Here's how to get started:
1. Personalize your profile
2. Upload your first photos
3. Find your friends on Flickr
   Or, learn more about contacts

The next page gives you three areas to fill out:

1. Create your buddy icon
2. Choose your custom Flickr URL
3. Personalize your profile

Buddy

First up is your "buddy" icon. The default buddy icon is a square gray smiley face. A lot of people never make a change to their default icon, so making an adjustment here can be one way of standing out from the crowd.

Below the smiley face on the right-hand side of the page is a link "Find an image on my computer." You can click here to find a suitable picture to upload. Three ideas for icons could be an item in your Etsy shop, a picture of you, or the avatar from your Etsy shop.

Once you upload your picture, the next page will direct you to create your buddy icon from your uploaded image. You can drag and resize the box that appears over your picture to frame your image, and I would keep the "constrain selection to square" checked.

Finally, click on "Make the icon," and the next page should show a green check mark with your new icon.

Flickr URL

Step two is "Choose your custom Flickr URL" and my advice would be to use your Etsy shop name and, as before, if it's already taken, try using a hyphen and so forth. This is an important step because once you've chosen your URL and submitted it, it cannot be changed.

For my example, my URL would look like this:

flickr.com/photos/seaglassjewelryboxexample

Profile

The "Personalize your profile" is the next step. Once you click on the link, you'll be taken to a page that asks for some basic information, e.g., first and last name, time zone, gender, and "singleness." The box below is vitally important because this is the only place on Flickr where you can really promote your shop (outside of the photographs you'll be uploading).

For the "describe yourself" field, you may wish to include a couple of lines about yourself and your Etsy shop, then, at the end of your text, copy and paste in your Etsy shop URL. You can also include a link to your blog or any other Web site that you wish to promote.

Once you've finished on this page, click "Next."

Uploads

In the menu bar at the top of the Flickr page are a series of options. To upload your photographs, click on "You":

Now choose "Upload photos and videos."

The following page asks you to choose photos and videos. Before you upload, I would recommend creating a special folder on your computer for this purpose. You could create a folder called Etsy Flickr, find the various photographs you wish to share on Flickr, and simply copy and paste into the new folder. This makes finding and selecting your photographs a lot easier when it comes to uploading to Flickr (or any Web site), rather than having to hunt for them one at a time.

You should already have a number of photographs that you have used in your Etsy listings, so you could copy them into your Flickr folder for upload.

When you select your folder from the upload menu, you'll see your photographs listed. Rather than select one at a time, you can click "Control" and "A" for Windows or "Command" and "A" for a Mac to "select all," which is quicker than clicking on one picture at a time.

As your photographs upload, a graphic appears which shows the progress of your upload. You can also see the size of your images and this is important because at the time of writing there is a cap on the amount of space a free Flickr account can use. Your limit is 100mb per month, so image size is something to take into consideration. As soon as a month has passed, you can upload another 100mb's worth of images and so on.

If you plan to use Flickr extensively as a part of your marketing efforts then you might like to consider upgrading to a paid account for more storage space. However, for the purpose of this tutorial, a free account should be fine.

When you upload your photographs, they appear in the top of the box as shown above. You can see that these three photographs add up to 5.22mb, and you're allowed to use 100mb per month. If you have a paid account, you gain a lot more storage space plus other advantages, but for now 100mb should be fine.

Privacy

Underneath your photographs is a place to set Privacy. If you have a separate account, where you wish to share pictures with family and friends only, then this is a great option, but for this exercise you'll want to set this to "public" so as many people as possible get to see your work.

Finally click "Upload photos and videos" and you'll see an animated bar moving; this represents the progress of your upload, and the more photographs you're uploading, the longer this process can take.

Once your upload is completed, click on "Add a description":

Finished! Next: add a description, perhaps?

This takes you to a page where you need to add some tags.

As with Etsy, you need to use tags that people who may be interested in your creations will be searching under, and you might want to copy and paste the existing tags from your Etsy listed items with commas separating each tag. I'd also include Etsy as a tag, as well as your shop name. You can add up to seventy-five tags with each of your photographs with Flickr, so if you have more than the fourteen tags used on Etsy feel free to add more!

To get an idea of popular tags, as well as "hot tags" being searched for at any time, visit:

www.flickr.com/photos/tags/

Title and Description

Each photograph should have its own title, and you could use the same titles that you have used in your Etsy shop. There is also a box for description, and, again, to save time, you could copy and paste the text from your Etsy listings, with a slight rewrite for anyone who visits your Etsy shop just so they don't end up reading exactly the same text when they glance through your listings.

Below the description box, the tag field should now be populated with the tags you entered in the earlier exercise.

Once you've finished with your titles, descriptions, and tags the right-hand side of the page gives you an option to "Add to a set." A set is a way of grouping a set of photographs together using a shared heading and allows you to link your photographs. For instance, with my fictional Etsy shop I might want a set for "Sea Glass Necklaces" and another for "Sea Glass Earrings." You can create a new set by clicking on the link and naming it, for example, "Etsy Shop Photographs"—or any phrase that will make the set easy for you to identify. As you add more and more photographs, being able to identify your sets can be really useful.

Once you have created a set, whenever you upload further photographs you can choose to add them to an existing set (or create a new one) and this helps both with organization and for viewers who may want to see a certain set of items, rather than all your photographs. If you're selling different items, then it's worth separating them into their own sets.

Once you're finished, click "Save" at the foot of the page.

Photostream

You will now be taken to a page that will show your Photostream. Another way of accessing this page at any time is to click "You" at the top of the Flickr bar and then "Your Photostream."

You can sort through your items, and if there are any you wish to delete or edit at any point, "Your Photostream" is the place to make changes.

You can also see the time, date, and camera used to take your photographs.

Bookmark

To give your Flickr page a further boost, you can Stumble it with StumbleUpon and share it on Su.pr, Tweet, and Facebook in addition to sharing it on your blog (more on these techniques in the coming chapters).

Flickr has been designed with networking and sharing in mind. A good way of networking is to log in to Flickr and use the search bar to find photographs by other artists or crafters (or whatever describes your particular field), add their work to your gallery, and leave comments showing your appreciation, which will often be reciprocated.

Leaving comments for other people is a great way to make new friends, share your work with others, and contribute to this fantastic community.

ACTION STEPS

- Sign up for a Yahoo! ID.
- Open a Flickr account.
- Personalize your Flickr account by adding your Etsy URL to your profile.
- Upload your best photographs into Flickr and include tags and descriptions.
- Stumble your Photostream, share with friends and family, and get the word out.

We Love Etsy

AS THE NAME of the site suggests, We Love Etsy (WLE) is a Web site that has been designed for lovers of all things Etsy. WLE includes a lot of sellers among its numbers, as well as buyers. WLE is an excellent place to promote your shop while sharing tips and tricks with fellow sellers. This works in a very similar way to the Etsy forums, but one difference is there are more opportunities on your profile for people to find out all about you.

Sign Up

To sign up, visit:

etsylove.ning.com/

Click on "Sign Up" on the right-hand side of the page and you will be taken to a sign-up page where you need to supply an e-mail address, set a password, and enter your date of birth. Finally, fill out the CAPTCHA and click "Sign up."

The next page requires you to enter further details, and you should take the time to include as much information as possible. You can upload a new profile picture or, for the sake of consistency and simplicity, use your existing Etsy avatar.

There are also places to include your Web site/blog or Twitter account, and because these are included in future lessons, you may want to make a note to revisit this page.

You can also include your new Flickr address, which was covered in the last chapter. If you're uncertain of your Flickr URL, you can find it by logging in to Flickr, clicking on "You" from the top menu, and choosing "Your Account" from the drop-down. You then need to scroll down to "Your Flickr Web Addresses" and copy your Photostream URL, for example:

flickr.com/photos/seaglassjewelryboxexample

You can also include links to Etsy teams you've joined, which is a great way to raise their profile and connect with other Etsy team members. The next box requires you to fill out an "About me," where you can include a brief bio.

The last box asks for a list of your Etsy favorites, which is where you can include fellow Etsy sellers and shops that you may have added to your favorites on Etsy. If you haven't added sellers to your favorites yet, it's worth visiting Etsy and finding a few interesting shops and then copying their URLs to fill out in WLE. This shows you are a member of the Etsy community, and community is the idea behind WLE, rather than just using the site for self-promotion.

Flickr

You can add videos and photographs to your page whenever you want, and it's a good idea to keep your page updated to keep it looking fresh and to show visitors your latest works. To update your page, log in to WLE and click on "My Page" from the main menu.

If you scroll down to "My Photos," you can click on "Add Photos," and rather than having to upload them from your computer, you can automate this through Flickr. To do this (you need to be signed in to Flickr in another tab in your browser) simply click on "Add photos from Flickr" and give the Flickr application permission to interact with WLE. Once you have granted permission, WLE will take the latest pictures from your Flickr Photostream and upload them to your page.

Etsy Mini

Now your basic profile page is ready, you need to add items from your Etsy shop, and you can do this really easily by using your "Etsy Mini."

Etsy Mini is a widget that allows people to see thumbnail previews of your Etsy shop, and you can add it to a variety of places, including your Web site (or blog) as well as Facebook. For this exercise you can add it to your WLE page by visiting your Etsy shop and signing in and under "Your Etsy" scrolling down to the "Promote" box and clicking "Etsy Mini":

You can try a variety of different options to find the one that works for you. A preview of your Etsy Mini appears below the option box as you make changes, which is really handy. Here are the settings I use:

1. **Items to show**—"Items from my shop"
2. **Choose image size**—"Thumbnail" (75px square)
3. **Choose layout**—5 Columns, 5 Rows

Below the preview of your Etsy Mini are two boxes: one allows you to copy code from the "Java-script" option; the other allows you to copy code for "Flash." For this exercise, copy the code from the "Flash" box by right-clicking and copying or pressing "Control" (or "Command" for Macs) and "C."

You can add the code to the "text box" in your WLE page and your items will now be showing, which gives visitors to your profile an instant preview of your creations.

Friends

The next step is to start interacting with fellow WLE members, and by doing so you will find people sending you friend requests and leaving comments on your page. This ability to interact with other sellers and artists makes WLE a fabulous resource.

A simple way to find people with similar interests to you is by clicking on the following tabs in the menu bar: "Members," "Photos," "Videos," "Forum," "Groups," and "Blogs." As you click on each of these tabs you are presented with a search bar and you can then run a search using keywords to find members making similar items.

As you discover people's pages, it's always worth leaving a friendly comment or compliment, and within the space of a few days you'll notice people visiting your page and doing the same. This is the best way to make new friends within the community, and, you never know, friends may in turn become customers.

Using the same tactic that was mentioned in the Etsy forums chapter, visit the WLE forums and look for posts to contribute to or answer people's questions. This will increase your visibility within this valuable networking site.

ACTION STEPS

- ☐ Sign up for a We Love Etsy account.

- ☐ Include all of your Web sites within your profile (adding in your new Flickr account).

- ☐ Add an Etsy Mini to your WLE page.

- ☐ Find other artists, crafters, and designers and say "hi," ensuring you leave them compliments on work that you appreciate and enjoy.

- ☐ Make a note to add the YouTube video, which you're going to learn to create in chapter 32, to your WLE page.

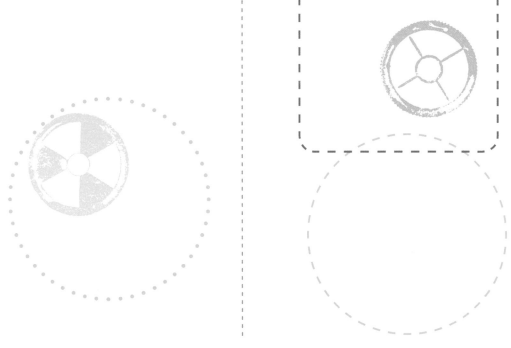

Getting ideas from Google Reader

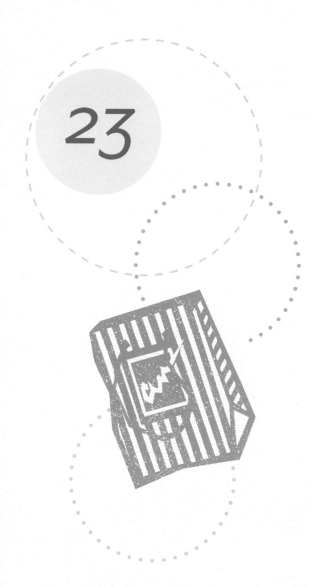

23

IN THE FOLLOWING lessons you're going to be creating a number of accounts with a variety of Web sites, where you can set up your own pages and add content to inform and entertain people who share an interest within your niche.

Using Facebook and Twitter, you will be sending out targeted messages to your audience, and while some of these are going to be your Etsy items, you will need to mix these self-promotional messages with news and other content.

Finding content to share and discuss on your blog and within these Web 2.0 sites may sound intimidating—what are you going to discuss? How are you going to find fresh news to share with others within your niche? How are you going to write articles and content? Luckily, there is an incredibly simple solution to these questions: Google Reader.

The following lesson is one of the most important in this book, because establishing an active presence on the Internet requires you to create lots of new content, and using Google

Reader will give you a simple way to find fresh content each day you wake up!

To get started, log in to your new Gmail account and then visit the following link:

www.google.com/alerts

This will take you to a basic search as shown below:

There are a few options with Google alerts; the first one is the keywords you wish to search for, and my example of "Sea Glass Jewelry" would probably not fit within this scenario, as it's likely the results this will return will be for other people's sea glass jewelry. While there's nothing wrong with helping fellow sellers, it's not going to promote your sales, which is the purpose of this book.

Keywords

You may be making items within a niche where you could find a wealth of alerts to share with your Twitter followers (as well as Facebook fans and people who follow your blog); for instance, if you typed "Photography" or "Fashion" into the alerts box there will be lots of results.

If, however, you're in a niche similar to sea glass jewelry then you can go a little wider in your search; perhaps try "Sea Glass." There may not be many stories, but occasionally you will receive an alert for this topic. Another alert, which will help to cast your net a little wider and find a variety of topics of interest for your potential audience and customers, would be "Etsy." Finding and sharing up-to-date info about handcrafted news and items can really help to set you up as someone "in the know" in the handcrafted niche.

To see how your alerts will look, type in your search phrase and click "Preview results."

Changing "Type" allows you to narrow down your options; perhaps you only want "News" or "Discussions." If you leave it on "Everything" while you're starting out, you can get a good feel for the types of content that will suit you.

The "How often" choice has three options. My personal preference is "once a day," and a good exercise is to check your alerts in the morning and then choose which ones you want to bookmark on Su.pr (which then distributes directly to Twitter and Facebook) or which stories would make good material to write a short commentary about on your blog.

"As-it-happens" is a great choice if you really want to stay on top of things, but it could lead to your in-box getting full quickly and this could be overwhelming. "Once a week" means you could miss out on current things to send out on Twitter (more on Twitter in Chapter 24) and you may find other people have already tweeted about them within your niche.

"Volume" has two options: "All results" or "Only the best results." Because I would worry about missing out on potential updates using the latter option, I set my Google Alerts to "All results."

Distribution

Your last choice is how you want to receive your alert. The default option is your Gmail address or "Feed." I prefer the feed option and use Google Reader, as covered below.

Once you begin to receive alerts, you need to decide which ones are worth writing about and which ones you would like to pass on to your followers on Twitter and Facebook. When you pass on information to your Twitter followers and Facebook fans, it's a really quick process, and after a few days you will get a good feel for how to use content in your Google Reader.

Google Reader

If you choose "Feed" from the "Deliver to" options, you can view your alerts in Google Reader. Please note it may take twenty-four hours for items to start filtering into your Reader. If you choose the "as-it-happens" option, then, depending on the popularity of your niche, items may appear almost immediately.

To access your Google Reader, go into your Gmail account and click on "Google Reader" from the menu at the top of the page.

I recommend setting Google Reader to show items in a "List" rather than "Expanded," as it makes skimming through items to post and share a lot easier, and when you start receiving twenty a day this feature helps avoid information overload:

Show: Expanded - List

show details

As you find stories of interest, there are a few options, and I recommend taking the time to explore Google Reader thoroughly, because it has so many benefits and it's invaluable for helping you find new content and establishing yourself as an authority on almost any topic.

A great way to gather content to share is by

using the "Add star" feature, which is a way of bookmarking with Google Reader and highlighting stories of interest that you may wish to return to at a later date:

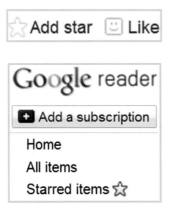

The second resource, which is helpful for use in combination with Twitter, Facebook, or a host of other social media sites, is the "Send to" function.

At the time of writing, this option is not included in the default Google Reader options, so we need to add it. To do this, you need to click on "Settings" at the top of the page and then "Reader settings":

From the far right-hand side of the "Settings" menu, click on "Send to" and you will see the following options:

There are a number of services you can "Send to." This means that as you find stories of interest, you can click "Send to" and it will automatically forward the stories to your social media sites and blogs. From this list I would select Twitter, StumbleUpon, and Facebook, as they are featured in this book. By selecting these services I can now post directly to them from my Google Reader.

Twitter

As mentioned, Twitter is going to be covered in full in Chapter 24, so you may wish to make a note to return to this chapter after you have set up your Twitter account following the tutorials in this book. For now, I'm going to use Twitter as an example of how you can distribute news from Google Reader to your various social media sites.

When you find a story you wish to share with your Twitter followers, simply click "Send to" in the dialogue box below the alert and choose Twitter (for this example).

This will take you directly to Twitter, where you will need to enter your Twitter username/e-mail and password. Signing in with Google Reader will automatically fill out the tweet for you, using the headline of the story and shortening the URL, which is a really handy feature.

Because the headline may be truncated, unless it flows for the people reading I recommend that you rewrite the text yourself and then, when you're satisfied, click "Tweet."

This method is a really quick way of getting out content to your followers, showing yourself to be an authority on a subject, and ensuring your tweets are well balanced and not purely self-promotional.

The other way of achieving the same result but also building up your StumbleUpon and Su.pr profiles is to find the news stories in Google Reader, copy URLs of interest, and then send them out by either clicking "Like" in your Stumble-Upon toolbar or pasting them into Su.pr and distributing them through their site. The advantage of mixing it up a little is so that you provide all sorts of content within your niche throughout the social media sites you're going to be using. This can help your accounts to avoid being flagged as spam by making too many self-promotional posts.

You can also add your Etsy feed to Google Reader and choose items from your shop to automatically post to your Twitter and other social media pages.

To do this, go to your Etsy shop (or any Etsy shop of interest) and click on "Actions" on the bottom left-hand side of the page, then click on "Subscribe to feed":

Provided you're already signed in to your Google account, you will be taken to a page that gives you the option of "Add to Google Homepage" or "Add to Google Reader," which I recommend.

Once you add your Etsy shop feed, it will appear in your Google Reader Subscriptions box:

Google Reader is an amazing resource and one I would use for finding fresh news to share with my online audience. There are many chapters in this book that will require creating content for various services, including Squidoo and EzineArticles, and Google Reader is a great place to start.

Sometimes when I mention using Twitter or Facebook to people, they roll their eyes and tell me they don't have time for all that "social media stuff"; however, using this method means you can keep up with your niche and provide interest to followers, fans, and potential customers, and all inside ten minutes or so each day.

ACTION STEPS

- ☐ Set up a Google alert within your niche and add to Google Reader.
- ☐ Become familiar with Google Reader and its various options.
- ☐ Set up Google Reader to submit to Facebook, StumbleUpon, and Twitter.
- ☐ Add your Etsy shop feed to Google Reader.

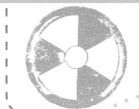

Of Tweeting and Twitter

24

WHILE MANY PEOPLE are familiar with Twitter, it can be confusing working out how to use Twitter in conjunction with your Etsy shop or online business. There are huge benefits to Twitter, but as with most lessons covered in this book, the key to building a successful presence is providing interest and value and not simply using social media for purely self-promotional purposes.

Twitter is best described as a micro-blogging platform where you're limited to 140 characters whenever you post an update (or "tweet"). Being limited to 140 characters may sound restrictive, but it works well, and the best way to get the most from this "limitation" will be covered in this chapter.

Twitter is more than simple updates; it's also a great way to interact with fellow crafters and prospective customers in real time, offering advice or posting links as and when questions arise.

At the time of writing, Twitter has over 100 million registered users, with approximately 300,000 new users joining every day. Twitter receives 180 million unique visitors per month, with over 600 million search queries per day. As you can see, Twitter is a colossal community with growing potential.

Setup

To set up a new Twitter account, visit:

twitter.com/

As before, I recommend you keep your "business" and "personal" Twitter accounts separate, so if you have an existing account, set up a new one for your Etsy shop.

Click on the large "Sign Up" button. The first thing Twitter will ask you for is your full name, and once it is entered a green check mark appears next to the box.

The next step is providing your username. Ideally, you would use your Etsy shop name, but if this is unavailable, you could add a couple of digits or use an underscore. After this, you will need to set your password and this needs to be six characters or more.

Next is your e-mail address, and for this I suggest using the e-mail address that I hope you have set up for your Etsy shop, rather than your personal e-mail address. If you add further Accounts at a later date, each one will need to have a unique e-mail address.

You can also read the "Terms of Service" and "Privacy Policy," and by clicking "Create my account" you confirm you agree with Twitter's terms.

The next screen provides you with suggestions of people you may wish to follow; I would ignore this for now and find people to follow who directly interest me.

Sometimes you see people with thousands of followers, and unless they're a celebrity or a known name this can be confusing—how did they find all these followers? They are often using a simple trick: they follow as many people on Twitter as possible in the hopes they'll follow them back!

This works and when people glance at your profile and see you have thousands of followers, it can make you look incredibly popular. The problem with this tactic is if you follow hundreds or thousands of people, then you will potentially miss the tweets (or messages) of the people you really do wish to follow.

Some people use automated scripts or "bots" to randomly follow people who they believe may be interested in the things they are selling, but this is not the purpose behind Twitter and is often a short-term tactic that can lead to more problems than benefits.

So, for now, skip this step, because later in this chapter you're going to discover how to find relevant people to follow, i.e., people with an interest in Etsy and arts, crafts and creativity.

Settings

You can adjust or change your settings at any time by choosing "Settings" from the Twitter menu.

The next page is your "Account Details." The first box allows you to change your Twitter username. However, I recommend that once you've chosen a relevant Twitter name to promote your Etsy shop, keep it rather than make changes, as this might confuse your followers.

You can also enter your time zone, which is worth adjusting, and there's also an option to "protect my tweets," which means that anyone who isn't following you cannot read your updates. If this was your personal account then this option might be worth checking, but because the exercise of this chapter is to promote yourself it's best to leave this field empty.

Once you're finished with this page, click "Save."

The next tab in the "Settings" menu is "Password," which allows you to change your password at any point should the need arise.

The next tab is for "Mobile," and this is where you can link your mobile phone to your Twitter account. I choose to skip this option, although this is purely a personal preference.

Notices

Next is "Notices," which gives you three options. The first is "New Follower Emails." I would leave this unchecked, because while initially it can be a novelty to receive updates each time someone follows you, over the course of time it can lead to your e-mail in-box becoming cluttered. Again, this is a personal preference.

Checking "Direct Text Emails" is a good idea; if someone is trying to contact you, then it's really helpful to be notified ASAP.

The last choice is "Email Newsletter," which is a handy way to receive tips and updates from the Twitter team. Once you check or uncheck your preferences, click "Save."

Bio

The next item on the "Settings" menu is "Profile." The first option is to add a picture; this needs to be under 700k in size, and unless you want to use a brand-new picture, I recommend uploading your Etsy avatar. As with the Etsy forums, each time you make an update your picture will show, so it's a good idea to use an eye-catching image.

You can also add your name, to make your tweets and conversations on Twitter more personal, and your location, and there is an empty space for "Web" where I recommend adding your Etsy shop's URL or Web site address.

The next box asks you for a "Bio." You have 160 characters to sell yourself, so it's best you take some time to consider how to best self-promote your work and intrigue people into following you, as well as enticing them to click on your Web site link.

A good way to start your bio is with something like "I am..." and then go on to describe your work while adding keywords that may help people find you easily.

For example:

> I am an avid artist and jeweler and specialize in working with Sea Glass Jewelry and have a passion for all things Etsy, vintage cars, and tightrope walking.

This description is 156 characters, which means I could use another 4 if I wanted to add a further keyword, for instance.

The point of adding in something like tightrope walking is to insert a bit of spice or interest into the bio. While making your bio purely professional has its benefits, injecting a bit of humor or eccentricity can liven things up a little.

I also used a few keywords in my bio, which will help people running Twitter searches (more on this later); the keywords used are "artist," "jeweler," "Sea Glass Jewelry," "Etsy," "vintage cars," and "tightrope walking."

Using keywords is a great way for people to find and follow you on Twitter. When you're finished here, click "Save" at the foot of the page.

Design

The next tab on the settings box is "Design," and this is where you can change the appearance of your Twitter page. This is something worth spending time on, because even though your tweets and updates are the main focus for your followers, a great-looking Twitter page is definitely an asset, and when it comes to selling, appearances are vital.

An additional reason to change your background is to give your page its own identity and to stand out from the crowd.

You can choose one of the theme templates that Twitter provides or you can use an image from your computer by clicking on "Change background image" and browsing for a suitable photograph or picture on your hard drive.

If you're proficient with design, then you can create your own custom Twitter background, and a simple search through the search engines or YouTube will bring you a host of tutorials. Another option is to pay someone a fee to make a custom background for you.

You can find designers on Etsy and fiverr.com and have a specially designed background made featuring your items, or if you simply type "Custom Twitter Background" into a search engine you will find plenty of ideas.

It may take some time to get a custom background specially made for you, so in the meantime, simply choose one of the free backgrounds provided by Twitter.

As well as changing your background, you can also change your "Design colors" in the "Design" options. This is where you can change the color of your hyperlinks, text box, and sidebar.

Once you're happy with your design, click "Save changes."

Connections

After you've been using Twitter for a while, you may find that you want to allow external applications to post to your Twitter account for you, and one example of this would be Su.pr, which was covered in chapter 21.

The advantage of granting Su.pr access to your Twitter and Facebook accounts is that you only need to post to one place. Su.pr will then post to both Twitter and Facebook for you, saving you the hassle of logging in to each separately.

To try this, head back to Su.pr:

su.pr/

Click on "Settings" and add Twitter, filling in your Twitter log-in and password, and then grant Su.pr permission.

Now it's time to make your first tweet, so grab a link that you wish to post, and a good one to use would be an item from your Etsy shop. So visit your Etsy shop, click on one of your items, and then copy the URL and paste it into the "Su.pr" box.

Once you click "Just Shorten" you can add text to encourage people to visit your URL, and then click "Post." Your message and URL will be sent to your Twitter account and broadcast to everyone who visits your Twitter page or follows you.

You can also set Su.pr to post to your Facebook account, which is another great feature in Su.pr. Facebook is covered in Chapter 26, and once you have set up your account you may wish to choose this option as well.

Allowing Su.pr access to your Twitter account means that a new tab will open in Twitter within your "Settings" box titled "Connections" and you will see the Su.pr icon. You can revoke access to your Twitter account by any third-party application through "Connections" whenever it suits you.

Followers

Now you have your account set up and have sent your first tweet, through either Su.pr or Twitter itself, it's time to find some people to interact with, and the easiest way to do this is by using the "Find On Twitter" function in the Twitter menu.

There are a few ways of doing this, but for the purpose of this chapter the two I suggest are "Browse Suggestions" and "Find On Twitter."

"Browse Suggestions" is helpful if you want to examine the various categories on Twitter and look for interesting people to follow in a whole range of different subjects, but "Find On Twitter" is the easiest to start with and is a more concentrated search:

Find accounts and follow them.

| Browse Suggestions | Find Friends | Invite By Email | Find On Twitter |

You can find people, organizations, or companies you know that already have a Twitter account.

Who are you looking for?

etsy

Examples: Bill, Bill Smith, or Whole Foods

Search

Running the above search brings up Etsy at the top spot, and at the time of writing they have over a million followers. Following Etsy is a good way to keep up with all the latest news. Another idea is to click on their "followers" and browse through and see if there are any fellow artists and crafters of interest.

You could also type in the keyword that relates to your Etsy shop and find more people to follow.

Often when you follow people on Twitter, you'll find they follow you back and gradually your followers will increase. You can also add your Twitter address within your Etsy shop an-nouncement and share it with family and friends, as well as including it on promotional items, such as the postcards or notes you use when you ship your Etsy sales.

Another resource for finding real-time Twitter updates is Twitter Search:

search.twitter.com/

This brings up a search box rather like Google, and you can enter your keyword phrase and find people discussing items of interest. You can then choose to follow them or perhaps "retweet" their messages, which is another wonderful way to break the ice and find new people to interact with.

Retweeting

Retweeting is very much like receiving an SMS text message and forwarding it on to friends and family in your cell phone's address book. Your motives for retweeting should be the same, i.e., to entertain or bring value to the recipients.

There are two main benefits to retweeting, the first being that if someone notices you're forwarding on their tweets they may follow you and retweet your messages. Second, you're providing value to your followers without having to come up with fresh content to send out. This is a useful exercise and can really help build your Twitter presence.

I would always ensure that the tweets I forward are of value.

You may know people who send out awful jokes or chain-letter messages to all and sundry, and if you're anything like me, you end up deleting their e-mails before you've even read them. This can easily be avoided by only sending out targeted tweets or retweets to your followers.

It's possible that you also know someone who seems to find the best jokes or Web sites and when this person forwards them to you, you can't wait to read them. This is simply down to editing, dismissing mediocre material and being selective in what you choose to send to people. The same applies to Twitter.

To retweet someone's message while logged in to Twitter, click on "Home," and this brings up your Twitter stream (the strip down the middle). Providing you are following people, messages should start appearing as soon as people post their updates. Simply hold your cursor over a message so that it's highlighted and then click "Retweet."

Direct Messages

You can direct message (DM) people whom you are following, and who follow you, directly from the Twitter interface. If someone makes a post and you want to send them a message, simply click on their icon and then click on the small cog to the right-hand side, which opens a small menu from which you can send a direct message.

When you send a direct message, you are lim-

ited to 140 characters, so if you wish to send someone a link, you may wish to use a URL-shortening service to give you the maximum amount of characters to play with. URL shortening is covered earlier, in Chapter 20 in the section on Su.pr.

When you receive a direct message, it shows on the left-hand side of your Twitter page as shown below:

Clicking on "Direct Messages" takes you to a page where you can read and respond to your messages as with your e-mail, only with a 140-character constraint.

Your "Direct Messages" box may fill quickly, and one reason for this can be "auto messages."

Auto Messages

Auto messages are automated responses that people set up to be sent out when you follow them. There are plenty of services on the Internet that will allow you to do this, but personally, I stay away from auto messages, and the reason for this is that they can be seen as a little "spammy"; for example:

Thanks for the follow; looking forward to your Tweets! Check out my site at———.

There's nothing wrong with the above message, but after you receive a few they begin to lose their impact and can also feel a little impersonal, which doesn't compel me to click on anything.

Not everyone uses auto messages for self-promotional purposes, but many do and these messages can soon clutter up your in-box, leading you to miss direct messages, which can then lead to valuable communications being lost. So this is why I choose not to use auto messages, and again, this is a purely personal preference.

Twitter Search

To make a real-time search of the latest tweets on any given topic, you can use the Twitter search box from the Twitter interface:

Once you have run your search, you have the option to save the details. This means that if you have a few searches of keywords of interest, you can simply click on them from your Twitter page and see all of the updates, comments, and questions for your niche:

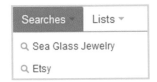

As you can see below, I set up a few searches for real-time updates on "Sea Glass Jewelry" and "Etsy," and by clicking on each of those links I get an instant overview on each subject. This is really handy if you want to find information quickly and connect with people asking questions within your niche.

For more advanced options, you can also visit Twitter Search:

search.twitter.com/

Using Twitter Search is a great way to stay up-to-date with all of the latest trends, respond to people's questions, and become a part of breaking conversations. You can also find great ideas for content for blog posts or articles (more on these later).

One thing worth pointing out is that even though you're using Twitter as a way to connect with potential contacts and buyers, there's no reason to stay within your niche. By looking at breaking topics and getting involved in all manner of conversations you'll begin to connect with a wide range of people, and this can be vital for the growth of your business, albeit in a subtle, passive way.

Rather than pushing your sales message, let people click on the URL in your profile and visit your Etsy shop for themselves and perhaps they'll bookmark it or suggest it to friends.

Promotion

Speaking of promotion, naturally you'll want to tweet about items in your shop, but personally, I would keep it at roughly a one-in-five ratio, i.e., four messages covering a range of interesting topics within your niche and one tweet for your Etsy items.

You can use Su.pr to tweet your items and get automatic feedback on how many people are clicking on them in both Twitter and Stumble-Upon. You can also see how many of your "sales tweets" are retweeted and by whom.

If people retweet your messages, it's worth sending them a quick DM thanking them, and if their tweets are of value and interest to your followers, retweeting their tweets equals social marketing!

Content

If you're going to be sending four non-promotional tweets for every one promotion, you need to find plenty of content to keep your followers entertained and interested. You can do this easily by using the techniques covered in the Google Reader chapter. Simply find news within your niche and then click "Send to" and send to Twitter, or copy and paste URLs of news stories and items of interest into Su.pr, which will then distribute to your Twitter and Facebook audience.

Humor

Besides tweeting about news stories within your niche, as well as your Etsy items, if you find a humorous story or video and you think it will entertain people, then tweet it! There are no hard-and-fast rules with social media; it all comes down to common sense.

Tools

Fresh and exciting tools are constantly being developed to improve the Twitter experience, and the majority are completely free. If you type "Twitter Tools" into Google and choose "Search by date," you can find the latest applications. Using applications and third-party tools is not only a fantastic way of improving your Twitter page; it can also really make your Twitter page stand out from other people's.

One tool that is indispensable when it comes to Twitter is TweetDeck, which you can download by visiting:

www.tweetdeck.com/

TweetDeck enables you to monitor tweets from people you follow, as they happen, and you can also see "mentions" (each time someone mentions your Twitter username on Twitter) as well as direct messages, and all-in-one interface.

TweetDeck is user-friendly and makes responding to incoming messages simple.

To get started, install it on your PC, Mac, iPhone, or iPad and fill out your Twitter username and password. I also recommend clicking on the "Remember me" option.

When you first open TweetDeck, you'll get a welcome screen that shows you various tips and tricks on getting started.

I recommend you click on each of the tip links, which connect you to Web pages offering further help. Two options which I would consider you click on are "Composing a message" and "Sort your information into columns."

Initially, when you open TweetDeck, it will set up default columns that allow you to get an overview of your account, and you can add or close columns at any point from the menu at the

top. It's definitely worthwhile to take a little time experimenting with the layout until you find the best fit for your monitor.

You can also compose messages within TweetDeck by clicking on the "Compose" button:

When you're composing a message, TweetDeck automatically shrinks your URLs for you, and there is a further feature that makes tweeting a breeze—TweetShrink! "TweetShrink" is the second icon from the left below the area for composing your messages. It has been designed to automatically shorten text in your messages to free up space. TweetShrink works by using abbreviations to free up characters in a similar way to how people abbreviate in their cell phone messages.

Another useful feature is being able to schedule your tweets:

Scheduling your tweets is a good idea if you find an interesting story to share, but perhaps it's late at night or the weekend or just a time when your followers may miss your update. This feature means you can choose when your update goes out.

Going back to Su.pr, they actually provide you with a suggested time to make your tweets in order to reach the most people, calculated by the amount of clicks you receive and when they occur. It's a good idea to check with Su.pr for your optimal time to post.

TweetDeck has masses of tools and options and I recommend you explore each of them to ensure you get the most from your Twitter experience. If you type TweetDeck into YouTube, you can find some excellent tutorials.

One last tip for finding all the latest tools and applications to improve your Twitter experience and stay ahead of the curve is to periodically run a search on Google for "Twitter Applications" and then click on "More search tools":

You can then click on "Past month" or "Past year," for example, and choose a custom range:

This is a helpful way of finding all the latest updates from Twitter applications on any subject of interest, and is a fantastic way to stay up-to-date on the Web.

There is a lot of information to digest in this chapter and you may need to return to it a few times as you build your Twitter presence. By following the suggestions outlined, you should find your Twitter experience is a lot more positive and fruitful than people who purely use it for sending out tweets about their Etsy items do. Over time, sales messages can become the virtual equivalent of white noise, but by using Google Reader and sharing news and fun stuff with your followers you ensure your tweets will stand out and your messages will be read.

ACTION STEPS

- Sign up for a Twitter account.
- Include your Etsy URL in your bio
- Design an eye-catching Twitter background.
- Send your first tweet.
- Find people of interest to "follow."
- Retweet other people's updates.
- Add a Twitter Search.
- Set up a TweetDeck account.
- Run a Google search for the latest Twitter applications.

Blogging—Your Online Diary

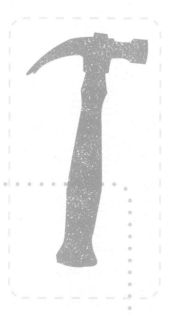

25

WHILE ETSY is fantastic for selling your creations, it's essentially an online shop, and therefore complementing your Etsy store with a second Web site can be an invaluable tactic to gain more exposure and lead more prospective customers to your shop. With your own Web site, you can post your thoughts, ideas, news, and tips and engage visitors through comments and articles.

You can set up a standard Web site surprisingly quickly using free online tools such as Mozilla's KompoZer, or if you have the time and money, Adobe Dreamweaver can help you create a sleek and professional Web site; however, there is a steep learning curve.

One of the simplest ways to establish a web presence without having to learn technical things such as HTML (Hyper Text Markup Language) or FTP (File Transfer Protocol) is to have a blog rather than a Web site; there are also plenty of free templates that can make your blog look like a more traditional Web site.

Advantages of a Blog

A blog has many advantages over a Web site. One key advantage is that search engines love fresh content and are more likely to rank Web sites that are regularly updated over "static" Web sites.

The very nature of updating a blog means you're adding new posts on a regular basis, very much like keeping a diary, whereas more traditional Web sites are often set up and populated with content and then receive irregular updates throughout the year.

Using a blog in conjunction with your Etsy shop means you can find a common way to engage with your customers and Twitter and Facebook followers. You can also post content about shared items of interest as well as posting entries showing your latest creations. Writing in your blog can also be a fantastic way of getting people excited about new projects you're working on, as well as allowing people to leave comments with constructive feedback.

As with Twitter, I recommend that you don't just make your blog a purely self-promotional vehicle and instead use Google Reader or Google alerts to find fresh content to write about and feature while interspersing this with your own work.

Free or Paid?

You can set up a free blog in next to no time. You simply choose the name of your blog and a template and start posting. There are a number of free blogs available, and these include Blogger (which is owned by Google), LiveJournal, and WordPress.com.

Advantages to using these services are mainly financial; essentially, you don't have to pay for your sites to be hosted and there are no other charges—they're completely free. Because they're owned by big companies, they're constantly being improved with security updates and new designs and templates. Indeed, your only real investment is time, and even this is minimal, as there is a fairly low learning curve.

But before you sign up for a free account and start blogging, I recommend considering the pros and cons of free versus paid and weigh your best options.

To my mind, the main disadvantage of setting up a free blog is one of ownership. You have next to no control over your blog and you're literally placing your writing and content on someone else's site. Some of the Web sites have some pretty strict rules over what they will allow and these terms and conditions can change, so you will need to stay up-to-date.

There have been cases where people's blogs have been closed due to being in breach of terms.

While these situations aren't the norm and you can often liaise with the companies hosting your blog, it's definitely something to take into consideration.

URL

Another disadvantage to using a free service is that your URL will end with the company's name, for example, seaglassjewelry.freeBlog.com. If you paid for your own hosting and URL, then you could have "seaglassjewelry.com" (if this domain name was available).

I don't want to put you off signing up for a free blog; there are huge advantages, but it's best to get the full picture and make a balanced decision.

If you choose the free option, then I recommend using the name of your Etsy shop as your blog title, and the same goes for buying your own URL.

If you wish to set up a blog with free hosting, then you can do so at any of these sites:

wordpress.com/
www.blogger.com/home
www.livejournal.com/

The next part of this chapter is dedicated to the steps you need to take if you decide to host your own Web site, as this is more complicated than signing up for a free blog account, although some of the same lessons apply in both instances.

Names

When you choose a name for your Web site you'll need to register it with a "domain registrar."

To choose the name for your Web site and check its availability, I recommend a Web site called Instant Domain Search:

instantdomainsearch.com/

As you enter the names that you'd like to register, Instant Domain Search begins to tell you if they're available as you type, which is a really handy feature. As you can see in the following illustration, seaglassjewelry isn't available as a .com (or .net and .org). There are other extensions for Web sites, such as .biz or .us, but as covered below, .com is usually the best choice.

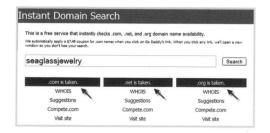

As in the illustration above, if your Etsy shop name is unavailable, then you might want to consider using a hyphen, Seaglass-jewelry, for example or a suffix or prefix, as in myseaglassjewelry, seaglassjewelryshop or seaglassjewelrybox. With a little imagination and patience, you'll find an available domain. Going back to my example shop, I modified my search to "seaglassjewelry-box" and as you can see in the below illustration, at the time of writing, the .com, net, and .org are all available.

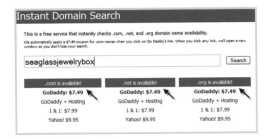

Once you've found an available domain it will need to be registered. There are a number of Web sites that offer this service, but I personally use GoDaddy.com, which can be accessed directly in Instant Domain Search by clicking on the link.

.com Versus .info

When you visit a domain registrar, you'll be presented with a number of choices and some of them will be a lot cheaper than the .com option. For example, at the time of writing you can buy seaglassjewelry.info for $.89 per year, as opposed to the $10.69 per year for seaglass-jewelry.com.

I would pay the extra and go for the .com option every time. Owning a .com has a more authoritative ring than owning a .info or other extensions. Also, a .com is a lot simpler for people to remember. If someone asks you for your Web site and you tell them it's seaglassjewelryshop.com, they're more likely to recall this than if it has a more obscure extension.

You can usually save money when you buy domains by checking to see if there are any coupon codes available; for example, run a search in Google for "GoDaddy coupon codes" and sort the results by date, choosing "past 24 hours" or "past week," et cetera.

You can also save money by registering your domain for a number of years rather than a year at a time, so if you plan to keep your shop open and build your brand for the long haul then this is something to consider.

Either way, I'd recommend ensuring the "Auto renew" box is checked, as this means you'll be notified and charged before your domain name elapses. This is important to avoid businesses that trawl the Internet looking for expiring domains that they snap up and then charge the former owner an extortionate fee to recover. I suggest you write yourself a reminder of the date you buy your domain (perhaps using Google Calendar) and ensure you pay for your domain's renewal in a timely fashion.

Hosting

Once you've purchased your domain name, you will need to find and pay a company to host your Web site. There are numerous options for hosting, and a lot of the larger companies will offer you hosting at highly competitive prices.

My own preference is a company called Host-Gator:

www.hostgator.com/

HostGator offers a number of packages, and if you are only going to own one Web site, I recommend the Hatchling Plan, which at the time of writing starts at $4.95 per month. If you decide to purchase and run a second Web site, then you can always upgrade to their Baby Plan, which starts at $7.95 per month, which is very reasonable, considering you can host as many Web sites as you like.

HostGator also has fantastic support, and you can chat with an advisor twenty-four hours a day, seven days a week, in "Instant Chat" and get free technical support.

Whichever hosting company you choose you can save a lot of time and effort if the host uses a service called cPanel, which is essentially a simplified control panel. The majority of cPanel might look complex, but for the purpose of getting your blog up and running within a few clicks, you can use a piece of software inside cPanel called Fantastico.

Fantastico installs WordPress on your domain with a "one-click" install, and there are plenty of videos on YouTube that will show you how to install WordPress both quickly and simply; just run a search for "How to install Word-Press using Fantastico."

If this is too complex or you do not have the inclination or time to install WordPress yourself, then typing "WordPress install" into a site such as fiverr.com will provide you with people who will do this for you for the princely sum of $5! You'll need to provide your log-in details for Host-Gator and your domain name, and once Word-Press is installed I'd change the log-in and password to protect my privacy.

You can change your account details at any point inside of WordPress Admin by going to "Profile" and then entering a new password. I recommend that whenever you use a site such as fiverr.com or anywhere that you pay for someone's services, you check the feedback and recommendations from other customers.

Themes

Once WordPress is installed on your domain, you will need to log in to your dashboard. This is the central area where you can add posts and control your Web site.

Usually the address to log in to your Word-Press account will be:

[yourwebsitename].com/wp-login.php

One of the first things I suggest is finding a "theme" for your blog, and there are two ways of doing this. The first is to run a search from within WordPress itself by clicking on "Appearance," then "Themes" in the main dashboard:

You can then click on "Install Themes" to find a theme for your site. When searching for themes, I look for three options. The first is "Two Columns"—this means you have one column for your posts and one on the side to add advertisements for your Etsy shop (or anything else you'd like to add).

The second option is "Right Sidebar," and this is where the graphics will go. This is just a personal preference; you can also have three columns or a left sidebar.

The third option is "Sticky Post," which I will cover on page 137. When searching for a theme, you can use the options at the top of the "Install Themes" to find the latest uploads. Three options are "Featured," "Newest," and "Recently Updated." It's worth taking the time to browse through each of these options until you find the best theme for your Web site. Personally, I like to

search for a theme that has a two-column format and a right-hand sidebar.

You can also find a larger range of themes in the search engines by typing "free WordPress themes." If you use Google, you can then "sort by date" so that you get the latest themes.

External Themes

Smashing Magazine is a wonderful site for finding elegant and unique themes and is definitely worth checking out for further options:

www.smashingmagazine.com/

You can either run a search within Smashing Magazine for "free WordPress themes" or type in "Smashing Magazine WordPress themes" into your search engine. Adding the current year to your search term returns the latest collections, as Smashing Magazine annually rounds up the year's best free themes.

Once you find a free theme that you like, download and save it to your computer (it should be delivered in a zip.file), then go back to WordPress and click on "Upload":

You can then upload the zip.file from your computer and the theme you chose will then be uploaded and installed.

The main thing to look for in a theme, apart from something that looks great, is to ensure it's "widget ready," which means you can add pictures and content to the "Sidebars" and place advertisements for your shop. You could make your own ads using a free service such as pixlr or visit Etsy or fiverr.com and request custom advertisements.

Widgets are incredibly easy to work with, and if you spend a little time on YouTube looking up "add image widget to WordPress page" you'll be an expert in no time!

First Post

The first post you create on your blog is the most important. When you make this first post, the search engines will visit your site and decide where it fits within their pages. Your first post needs to achieve a few things: First, it needs to be of a decent length, short enough not to be overwhelming for readers but long enough to show the search engines that your site is not "spammy" or a fly-by-night. I'd suggest your first post has a word count between two and four hundred. To make your first post, go to Posts and "Add New Post" as shown below:

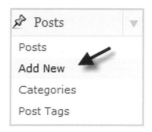

Within the first line you should include your keyword and shop name (which may be one and the same) and highlight it by using bold or italics, for instance:

> This blog is a showcase for my **Sea Glass Jewelry** and creativity and is designed to cover all manner of fresh and exciting innovations in the world of online crafts and jewelry making.

Using your keyword in each post and bolding or italicizing it is a potential way of drawing the search engines' attention to the theme of your content, as is using your keyword in the titles of your posts.

While you need to mention your keyword, make sure you avoid "keyword stuffing" (overuse of your keyword in your text). Besides making text awkward to read, keyword stuffing can cause the search engine robots to "de-index" guilty sites, which can lead to your site disappearing from the search engines' index or receiving low rankings.

I tend to make most of my blog posts around one hundred words, following the sticky post (more information on page 137), and use my keyword once in the opening sentence (bolded) and once more in the closing paragraph or sentence (italicized).

Making keywords into anchor text (more on these to come) is really simple in WordPress, but I suggest keeping clickable links to a minimum to cut down on the amount of people leaving your site; however, you can set clickable text to open a page in a new browser window. Something to bear in mind is that the "authority" or importance of your Web site (and therefore how high it ranks in the listings) is measured by the amount of links coming *to* your site rather than leading out.

I've given my first post the title "Sea Glass Jewelry Creations" and pasted in my text, which is just a snippet for illustration purposes. If this were a real post, then the length of this article would be between one and three hundred words.

To set text to bold or italics click on the icons highlighted in the image below:

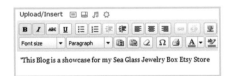

To make text into a link click on the chain-link icon indicated by the red arrow in the following illustration.

When you click on the chain-link icon, a further box appears:

You will then need to enter the link to the site you wish to direct people to in the link URL field. I set the "Target" to "Open link in a new window," which I hope means people will stay on my site longer, and also because I don't want my visitors to read my articles, click on a bolded link, and have the annoyance of being taken off page from the article they are reading.

The "Title" you use is important and should match the text that you've highlighted; in this case, it's "Sea Glass Jewelry Box." This will make the text into anchor text and it helps the search engines understand what this article is about. This is also another way to strengthen your Web site for your keyword phrase, but again this should be used sparingly. I try not to include more than one anchor text link (or outgoing URL) per blog post. The final option of "Class" I leave as "Not set." The class option allows you to use CSS (Cascading Style Sheets) to apply effects, styles, and colors to your links, but for the purpose of this tutorial you can leave yours as "Not set."

As well as using anchor links to send visitors to your Etsy shop, if you write features about other people's content or Web sites you should always provide a link to their work or sites as a courtesy. It's also a good idea to contact people and let them know you've written about them and will remove the post if requested. Most of the time people are delighted to hear they've been featured, and they may even link back to your site, which is a real win-win situation!

So now that the text has been turned into a clickable link, it will be highlighted in blue:

"This Blog is a showcase for my Sea Glass Jewelry Box Etsy Store"

Pictures

You can also add images to your posts, which is a great way to break the text up and make it more appealing to readers. You can add pictures by clicking on the highlighted icon below:

You then need to select the image you wish to use from your computer; one tip is to make your image size as small as possible, ideally under 80kb.

You can find free services online that will shrink image sizes by searching for "reduce image size online" and then uploading files you wish to downsize, but always make sure you are uploading "copies" and not original pictures.

The more pictures you use and the larger their file size, the slower your Web site will load. It's worth noting that some people still use "dial-up" Internet, which means if you have a slow-loading site they may give up or click elsewhere. I try to limit each post to one image where possible.

Saving your images as GIF (Graphics Interchange Format) files is the best way to reduce file size while ensuring your image looks good on the Web.

When you upload your picture, you're presented with a few options:

First is your "Title." For my example, I would add "Sea Glass Jewelry Necklace." You can be as imaginative as you like, although you should try to include your keyword and also keep the description brief.

For "Alternate Text," you will want to slightly rewrite your "Title." My example would be "A necklace made from Sea Glass Jewelry." The idea for Alternate Text is for people who are visually impaired, so try to consider this when writing your description, but again, keep it brief.

Whether you want to use the Caption option

is up to you. This will place a caption below your image.

You can also add a "Description" for your image in case the image doesn't show in a Web browser. Sometimes this happens if people are using dial-up Internet and their browser struggles to load large images. I try to keep images for posting in WordPress to under 50kb in size (using Picnik) to avoid this, but having a description also acts as a safeguard for all eventualities. An example description for my picture could be "Pale blue sea glass jewelry pendant."

WordPress will add its own "Link URL," which will link to the image, unless you change the URL. On this occasion, I've added a link to my fictitious Etsy shop so if someone were to click on the picture they would be taken to my Etsy shop. I don't always do this; sometimes I leave the WordPress URL where it is to cut down on external links leading from my site.

I also leave the default image size at "Medium" and click "Insert into Post."

Your image will now show and you can preview your post along with the image by clicking on "Preview":

This gives you a good idea of how your post will look when it's published, and it's always worth previewing first to make sure you're happy with the formatting:

As you can see above, the text has wrapped around the image, and I prefer the image to rest above the text, so I'll reposition the picture by clicking on the "frame" around it:

Then I click on the "Align center" option:

As you can see by clicking "Preview" again, the picture has now moved and the post is far more "readable":

Sea Glass Jewelry Creations

Sea Glass Jewelry Necklace

"This Blog is a showcase for my **Sea Glass Jewelry** and creativity and is designed to cover all manner of fresh and exciting innovations in the world of online crafts and jewelry making."

The last thing to do before you publish is suggest which categories your post will appear in. To access the categories, head to your WordPress dashboard and click "Posts" and then "Categories" from the menu on the left-hand side of the dashboard.

You'll need to add some categories, so, for instance, I would add "Sea Glass," "Sea Glass Jew-

elry," "Sea Glass Necklace," and "Etsy," and so on. Categories are a great way for you to organize your blog, and people can click on your "Categories" and find the related content you post under each one.

You can also add tags which are another way to organize your content. While you can add as many tags as you like, I would ensure that they are relevant to your post and try not to add too many. Having accurate tags can help with Search Engine Optimization and I will usually use between five to ten tags for my posts. The option to add tags is below "Categories" on the right hand of your "Add New Post" menu.

Sticky Post

Sticky posts give you the option of creating a post that will always be at the top of your blog without moving down the page as you add new content. Most blogs work by featuring the latest post at the top of the page and older content gets pushed down the page over time. To add a sticky post go to your WordPress dashboard and click on:

I've chosen the "Sticky" option for this post, as I want it to be the first thing that visitors to my site read, as well as the search engines. All future posts will have the "Normal" option selected, which means they'll appear at the top of the site (below my sticky post) and will gradually be pushed down the site as newer posts appear.

Once you're finished with your sticky post and you're ready for it to appear online, simply click "Publish":

Your post is now live on the Internet!

You may notice that above the "Publish" button is an option preset to "Publish **immediately.**" You can change this, and there's a small calendar that will allow you to publish content in the future rather than immediately. This is a great help if you have a few ideas and wish to spend some time writing posts that you can then "drip feed" over time. If you know you're going on vacation or will be too busy to write blog posts, you can cue them ahead of time to automatically post when you're busy.

Once your post is published, I'd recommend giving it a Stumble and tweet, and after the next chapter, or if you're already familiar with Facebook, you could use Su.pr to rate and post your blog entry to Twitter, Facebook, and StumbleUpon in one click.

Pages

You can also add pages to your site, which means you could have a page dedicated to "Sea Glass Jewelry," one for "Sea Glass Necklaces," and one for "Sea Glass Earrings." You can have a multitude of pages, but they are different from your main blog page in that you cannot add posts to your secondary pages; however, you can add content to them whenever you please.

So if, for example, I created a new range of sea glass earrings I could go to my "Sea Glass Earrings" page and add new pictures as well as text. You can also add videos to any of your WordPress pages (creating videos is covered in Chapter 32), and adding fresh content to your pages is always a great way to bring the search engines to revisit your blog.

To create a new page, choose "Pages" from the left-hand menu in your dashboard, then "Add New".

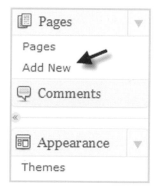

When you create blog posts on your main page, you can also link them to your other pages by using anchor text. This can help the structure of your Web site.

Links you create pointing back to your site will be of benefit and will help strengthen your Web site's authority on the Internet, so you should add your Web site URL wherever you get the chance, such as on Web 2.0 Profiles (covered in Chapter 29) or on accounts such as We Love Etsy and the other places featured in this book.

Of course Etsy should be your primary focus because that's your "money site," but wherever there is an opportunity to add another URL you can use your Web site and if you have additional pages you could always add these. For example, if you created a profile on a forum or group dedi-cated to necklaces, you could link to your "Sea Glass Necklace" page and this will mean the page will have a backlink from an external site.

WordPress is very powerful and you can use it in a variety of different ways. There are lots of ways you can improve your site, but this is be-yond the scope of this book. If you type "SEO WordPress" into YouTube, you'll find plenty of useful videos that will take you through optimiz-ing your WordPress blog for the Internet.

Plug-ins

Plug-ins are another good reason to use Word-Press. Plug-ins are small programs that can be added to your WordPress site, very much like ex-tensions. You can find a wealth of plug-ins within WordPress or by searching on the Internet.

If there is a service you use and would like to know if there is anything to integrate it with WordPress, simply run a quick search online. For example, if I type in "Twitter WordPress Plug-in" I get plenty of results, some of which mean that whenever I create a new post on my site Twitter will be updated. Because I use Su.pr I don't need this plug-in, but it's an example of how you can find different ways to extend your Web site.

Some highly useful plug-ins that I recommend installing are "All in one SEO Pack," which allows you to optimize your posts for the search engines; "Akismet," which is a great way of preventing people from spamming your blog; "WP-DB-Backup," which e-mails a copy of your WordPress Database to you so you can back it up and reload your site if the need ever arises; and "WP Super Cache," which speeds up the load times of your WordPress sites.

One note of caution is not to add too many plug-ins, as this could slow your Web site down. This can sometimes be difficult given all the new innovations being added to WordPress, but you can delete or deactivate plug-ins at any stage. One thing that is important is updating plug-ins when you receive notifications in your control panel, as these updates provide security fixes and improvements.

What to Post?

Once you've created your sticky post, you might wonder what to follow it with. A blank screen can be just as intimidating as a blank sheet of paper! Ideas for posts could be adding new items from your Etsy shop or plans for future items and ranges, plus using Google Reader or alerts to keep an eye out for news within your field and using this as a base for your own articles and blog posts.

I apply the same rule of thumb to my blog as well as my Twitter page: one in five promotional posts; however, this may be overly conservative and you need to find what works for you.

Another way of finding new content is to approach other Etsy sellers (as long as they're not direct competitors!) and see if they're willing to write a small piece about their work—or even answer a small Q&A or interview. Not only can this be an excellent way of finding new content for your blog, but you may also be approached to write something in return and receive a backlink to your site, and the more links that point to your Web site the better!

ACTION STEPS

- Decide between a free or paid blog. If you decide on a paid blog:
  - Buy your own URL (if you didn't choose the free option).
  - Set up hosting.
  - Install WordPress with Fantastico.
- Find and choose a theme.
- Create a sticky post.
- Add a picture to your first post.
- Create "anchor" text that links to your Etsy shop.
- Add tags and categories to your post (which can also be used in future).
- Add further pages if relevant for your blog.
- Find plug-ins to improve your site.
- Publish your first post.
- Brainstorm future posts.
- Write a future post.
- Aim to post to your blog at least once a week.

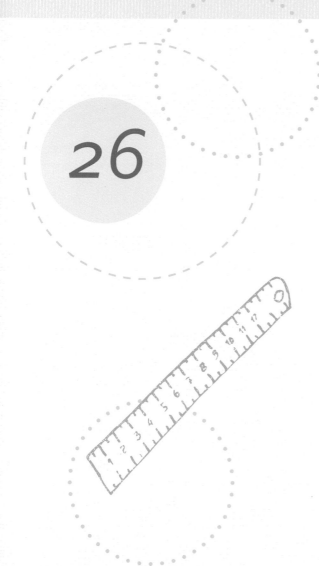

26

FACEBOOK has become a huge contender on the Internet, so developing a Facebook presence is absolutely vital for any business, and your Etsy shop is no exception.

People are turning to Facebook as a "one-stop shop" to chat with friends and family and share pictures, videos, and Web sites as well as socialize. At the time of writing, there are around 500 million Facebook users and the site receives around 260 billion page views per month.

Etsy has integrated Facebook and you can share your items without having to copy and paste the link into Facebook by simply clicking on one of your items in Etsy and "Share" under "Page Tools":

You can also post directly to Twitter, Stumble-Upon, and Tumblr, among other sites. This is a great way to post quickly and simply, so each time you post a new Etsy item you can automatically share it on your Facebook profile. However, I would continue to use Su.pr for this exercise, because it posts to Facebook, Twitter, and StumbleUpon in one hit and gives you really useful statistics.

As I write this chapter, you can't actually post to your Fan Page within Etsy, only your personal profile. This may be subject to change in the future. For the purpose of this chapter I'm going to be referring to your Facebook "Business" Page as your Facebook Page and your "Personal" Facebook Profile as your Personal Facebook Profile.

Sharing your Etsy creations within your personal Facebook profile can be helpful if friends or family share your items with their Facebook friends, but the purpose of this chapter is to discuss your Facebook Page rather than personal Facebook profile.

Your Facebook Page will be a dedicated page for your business and this means the way you interact, post, and share on your Facebook Page will probably be very different from the way you use your personal Facebook profile.

To create a Facebook Page, you will first need a personal Facebook page, so if you haven't set one up yet, then head to:

www.facebook.com/

The front page has an option to either login or sign up for a free account. You will need to fill in your details and set up a password and e-mail address. At this point I would use my personal e-mail address rather than my dedicated Etsy shop e-mail. This is so you can take some time to become acquainted with Facebook and find friends and family to connect with. Each time someone comments on your page or sends you a message, you'll receive an e-mail notification and it's best to keep these within your personal e-mail account so you don't miss any important notices.

When you're ready to set up your Facebook Page, log in to Facebook and visit:

www.facebook.com/pages/

On the next page, under the "Create a Page" menu, select "Create a Page for a brand, product, or organization" and then give your page name, in this instance "Seaglassjewelry." You will also need to confirm that you're the "official representative of this...business" by placing a check in the Facebook Terms box.

The first option on the next page is to add an image. As with the other chapters in this book, I recommend you use the same image that you use for your Etsy avatar in order to keep a sense of consistency and to establish your brand. This is my own personal preference but you may want to add a picture of yourself or one of your items.

The next option asks for some basic information on the year your company (or shop) was founded, which should be a straightforward answer. Clicking on "Detailed Info" brings up a large box where you can add more information. Within the "Detailed Info" you can include your Web site (enter your complete Etsy shop address, for example: www.etsy.com/shop/SeaglassJewelryBoxExample).

You can also include a company overview; here's one I used for my fictitious Etsy shop:

> I design jewelry from Sea Glass and natural materials and love finding nature's treasures washed up on the seashore!
>
> My Etsy shop was set up in Fall 2010 and has become my main outlet for creativity and sharing my passion for Sea Glass. I hope you will enjoy visiting my page and please feel free to contact me with any questions or suggestions!

I recommend you add text to the "Mission" box and keep it brief and relevant. For my page, I would add:

Fashioning jewelry from organic, natural materials

Finally, in the "Products" box you simply need to add the products you make: "Sea Glass Necklaces, Rings, Earrings, Bracelets, and Pendants."

When you fill out your company overview you will want to give prospective customers a good reason to join your Fan Page and, you hope, visit your Etsy shop, so I recommend taking a little time to create compelling copy. Once you've finished, click "Save Changes."

The next few fields on the "Get Started" tab allow you to post an update (you can make one now or wait until the page is ready). You can also set up your mobile phone if you want to post pictures and updates from your cell phone. Finally, add your Twitter account by linking it to your Facebook page.

Once you've added your info into "Get Started" you can add photos of your work by clicking on "+ Create a Photo Album." Here you can give your album a name, location, and brief description.

For my album, I will give it the name "Sea Glass Jewelry" and you should use a keyword for each album you create. For "Location" I would add "Etsy Shop" and finally under "Description" I would add some text that neatly summarizes my photo album, something along the lines of "Here are a few photographs showcasing pieces from my Etsy shop."

Once you've created your album, you can add photographs. These should be similar to the images you shared on your Flickr account, i.e., photographs showcasing your best items. To ensure you keep your account up-to-date, you could create a reminder in your diary or Google Calendar and log in once a month to add pictures of your latest work.

Once you've uploaded your photographs, you can organize or edit whenever you choose by clicking on "Edit Photos." This allows you to add a caption. "Add More" gives you the ability to add additional photographs to your album; you can use "Organize" to drag and drop your photographs and rearrange them, "Edit Info" changes the album name and details, and, finally, "Delete" does exactly what it says!

The bottom of the box gives you a URL, which is a direct link to your album, and you can share this on your Web site or in your Etsy shop announcement or forward it to your Twitter followers as well as socially bookmarking it for further exposure.

There are two ways of displaying Etsy items on your Facebook Page and it's worth using both. First, you can add a "My Etsy" tab by signing into Facebook and clicking on:

apps.facebook.com/myetsy/

Once you visit this page you can add a "My Etsy" tab to your Facebook Page.

First, click on "Add To My Page" and then visit your profile. The "My Etsy" icon should be showing on the left-hand side of your page under the "Wall" and "Info" options. Click on "My Etsy" from the left-hand menu and you will then be prompted to enter your Etsy username. Click on "Submit" and, on the next page, grant permission.

You will then be prompted to enter your Etsy username, then click "Submit" and, on the next page, grant permissions. The next step should now show the avatar from your Etsy shop, and it will also ask you if you want to show favorite items and sellers (I would click "no" for this exer-

cise). You can also add the feed from your blog or Etsy shop on this page.

An RSS (Really Simple Syndication) feed address will often be the name of the site followed by "feed." For example: seaglassjewelry.com/feed/. RSS feeds are a way for people to "subscribe" to Web sites and receive updated content without having to check if a Web site has been updated. RSS is covered in more detail in the upcoming Squidoo (Chapter 27).

If you prefer, rather than use your blog feed you could use your Etsy RSS by clicking on your Etsy shop and selecting your feed from the "Actions" menu by right-clicking on "Subscribe to feed," selecting "Copy link location," and then pasting into the RSS space in the "My Etsy" application. This will allow your Etsy items to appear in place of your blog feed, so people can see recently listed items. My preference would be to use the blog feed, as your Etsy items will already be appearring in you "My Etsy" tab, so you have an opportunity to show off your Etsy items *and* your blog posts.

When you click on the "My Etsy" icon on the front page of your Facebook page, you should now see a page featuring photographs and titles of Etsy listings.

To add "My Etsy" to your Facebook Page simply click back on:

apps.facebook.com/myetsy/

Then select "ADD TO MY PAGE." You will then need to choose your Page title from the

"Add this application to": drop-down. Click on "Add My Etsy" and follow the same procedures as above, adding your Etsy username, the favorites option, plus RSS feed address.

What's on Your Mind?

Now it's time to post some content to your front page, and just like with Twitter, you can post anything you like, even something so simple as a brief "hello." It's always good to try to keep the content posted to your Facebook Page as niche relevant as possible.

I would suggest you keep "personal" updates to a minimum on your Facebook Page. There's nothing wrong with posting something personal now and then, as it shows you are human, but for this exercise I'll show you how to use Facebook to promote your Etsy shop and/or Web site.

To make a post, make sure you're on your Facebook page and click on "Wall." You will now see a box that asks "What's on your mind?"

This is where you can post your updates and let people know whenever you create new items in your Etsy shop and share news or links that you think will be of interest to people who have "liked" your page. You can also attach links, photos, events, and videos within your message using the buttons just below the "What's on your mind?" dialogue box. Once you're happy with

your message and it's ready to be posted, simply click on "Share."

Using the same rule of thumb from previous lessons, I recommend you intersperse your sales messages with content that people will find of interest within your niche, using Google Reader.

Your page will look a little bare when you first start out, so it's a good idea to post a few topics of interest and share links to your Etsy shop, both as practice and to give your page some content and substance. This way, visitors will see that you are active and this may increase the chances of their "liking" your page and following your updates.

Address

Something that is worth taking a little time to customize is your Facebook Page URL. When you first set up your Page, it defaults to your page's name with random digits that can be difficult for people to memorize.

At the time of writing, you will need more than twenty-five people to have "liked" your page to be able to complete this step, so it's a good idea to write to existing friends and family on Facebook or your Twitter followers and perhaps post a new thread in Etsy offering to "like" other sellers in return for their "liking" your page. You can also skip ahead to the "Groups" part of this chapter to find ways to find and interact with other Etsy sellers and people within your creative niche. Start to communicate and "like" people, as they will often return the compliment.

Once you have at least twenty-five people who have "liked" your page, log in to Facebook and go to the following URL:

www.facebook.com/username/

Then click on "Set a username for your Pages."

You will then need to type in the name you wish for your URL and click "Check Availability." Something to bear in mind is that once you have confirmed your selection, you cannot change it at a later date.

You may find that someone is already using your desired username, so you could add a suffix or prefix. If "Seaglassjewelry" was taken, I might choose "Seaglassjewelryshop" or "Seaglassjewelry-box."

The key is to choose a name that includes your Etsy shop or the keywords you wish to be found for, i.e., "Sea Glass Jewelry," or preferably both.

Groups

An excellent way of networking with other sellers and people with a shared interest in your niche is joining Groups on Facebook. To do this, type in your keyword within the search box at the top of the Facebook page and you'll receive a number of mixed results, including individuals, Fan Pages, and Groups. To filter this down, click on "See more results."

Now you can choose the "Groups" option to narrow your search.

Once you find a relevant Group, simply click on "Join Group," and from there, depending on the Administrator's settings, you should be able to post content to the main wall exactly as you do on your Facebook wall.

As previously mentioned, you will want to keep the posts relevant to the Group and you can also "like" and comment on other people's posts, which is an excellent way to network and meet new people who will, you hope, come and visit your page and "Like" it.

To "like" someone's post and/or to add a comment or share, simply click in the "Like" box below their update.

Leaving a comment will show the original poster that you appreciate their content, as will clicking on "Like." You can also click on "Share," which will allow you to share the post on your own wall. "Flag" is for posts that you consider spam, but this exercise is about building relationships, so it's unlikely you will use this option while networking on Facebook.

The law of reciprocation can often come into force on Facebook, Twitter, and most social-networking sites. In other words, the more you contribute and leave kind and constructive comments for people as they share their ideas or interests, the more likely they will do the same for you.

Even though you're in the business of selling, again it's worth limiting your promotional posts, as it's unlikely that posting your items to a Group page will win you many "likes"; indeed, this is where people could potentially "Flag" your posts as spam.

The best way to look at Groups is as a place to communicate with other sellers and potential customers by piquing their interest through items you share and, in turn, they may well "Like" your Facebook Page and see your sales messages mixed in with your shared content.

Becoming an active member within your Group and sharing up-to-date news (using Google Reader or Google alerts) is a fantastic method to be seen as someone with their finger on the pulse, which can help to grow your own contacts and people who will visit and "like" your page.

Create Your Own Group

If there is no Group within your field, you can always start your own and search for users who list your keywords within their profiles and then send them invites.

To set up a Group, click on the "Groups" option in your home page (under "News Feed" in the left-hand menu and "more") and then "Create a Group." You will then need to answer a series of questions, including the Group's name and a brief description. As with the other lessons in this book, you'll need to sell your Group in this box and create copy that will encourage people to join.

Once you have filled in the various options and agree to the terms, click "Create Group," and from there you can upload a picture for your Group (try to use something eye-catching).

The next page gives you a series of options that are worth checking over. These are allowing (or disallowing) other members the options to post content, comments and photographs. Leaving the default options as they are and ensuring "Access" is set to "This Group is open" will allow people to participate within your Group, which is ideal for the purpose of this exercise.

Finally, click "Save," and on the next page you will be given the opportunity to invite people from your contacts list to join your Group. If you do not have any contacts yet, then participating in existing Groups will bring you into contact with all sorts of people and you can click on their names at any point and then "Add as friend" and, as long as they agree, you will start making new friends. As soon as people become your friends, you can click on the name of your Group from your home page and invite people in.

You can also change the logo or picture of

your Group (which defaults to a question mark) by clicking on the "?" icon.

This covers the essentials of marketing with Facebook.

You may notice that behind each of the chapters is essentially the same message: contributing and sharing as well as promoting your own items. The reason for this is simple: it works! Engage people, "like" what they do, and comment on their work and ideas and gradually, over time, you'll build up a small army of friends and followers. If people like your work, then there is a good chance they'll spread the word for you, bringing you free, organic traffic. Word-of-mouth advertising at its best!

ACTION STEPS

- ○ Sign up for a personal Facebook account.
- ○ Familiarize yourself with how other users interact on Facebook.
- ○ Create a Facebook Page.
- ○ Post an update to your Facebook profile as well as your Facebook Page.
- ○ Find twenty-five people to "like" your Facebook Page.
- ○ Customize your Facebook Page to a more reader-friendly URL.
- ○ Find or set up a Facebook Group that relates to your niche.

Creating a Lens with Squidoo

27

SQUIDOO is a free Web 2.0 site that allows you to create your own Web page, referred to as a Squidoo lens, within their network. You can share content relating to your niche with your audience and peers, as well as other members of the Squidoo community. This provides an opportunity to market and promote your Etsy items and videos of your work. There is a huge variety of topics on Squidoo, and quite apart from promoting your Etsy shop, it's a great resource to find all sorts of fascinating information.

Squidoo pages can rank really well within the search engines, because the community within Squidoo has created a vast network of valuable information relating to many topics of interest. So it's worth taking some time to build a presence within this fast-growing information-focused Web site. Creating content will be easy for this exercise, as you simply need to write about the work you sell on Etsy!

You can visit Squidoo at:

www.squidoo.com/

I would recommend taking a little time to browse through Squidoo and type in keywords of interest so that you can see how other people construct their lenses.

When you're ready to set up your own lens, you'll need to sign up for a new account, which you can do either through Facebook or through Squidoo's Web site. You will need to provide the usual details, including name, password, and e-mail address. You will then be sent an e-mail asking you to verify your account.

Bio

Once you have signed into Squidoo after e-mail verification, it's a good idea to set up your bio (this will be used for all of your Squidoo lenses). The first step is to add an image and edit your bio. Click on "Change Picture" to add an image, then "Edit Your Bio" to create your bio.

As mentioned in previous chapters, you could use the same image that you use as your avatar on Etsy.

Your bio is an opportunity to provide readers with a bit more background on you and your work. As well as adding in a personal detail or two, it would be helpful to include some brief information about how you came to make and sell and why you love working within your niche. Remember, enthusiasm is infectious, so you really want to pique people's interest in both you and your work.

Beneath your bio and picture is an area where you can include details about other Squidoo lenses that you own (if relevant) and, importantly, include external links—this is an invaluable area to populate and well worth taking the time to complete. Key details to include are your blog, Twitter and Facebook page, and Etsy shop.

If you browsed through Squidoo and found pages of interest, you can include other people's lenses in the space provided. This can be useful for people who visit your lens, particularly if these lenses are relevant to your topic or niche.

This page also allows you to change your account settings and time zone.

Once you have finished with "My Profile," click on "My Lenses" to make your first lens.

The first step is to tell Squidoo what your page is going to be about:

Step 1: What's your page going to be about?

The best pages are on specific topics, like 'how to roast your own coffee beans' or 'wheat free dog treats' or 'where to buy Star Wars bedsheets!' What do you want to write about? Be specific!

My page is about:

[Continue »]

3 steps remaining

The next page will ask you for a title for your page and provide you with a preview of how your URL will look. You will then be asked to choose both a category for your lens and a rating (G rated is the default and means it's suitable for all ages).

Once you hit "Continue," if the title for your page is available you will be able to carry on through the process, but if not, you may get a message letting you know the lens name has already been taken. If this is the case you can try variations. For instance, if "Sea Glass Jewelry" is taken, try "Sea-Glass Jewelry" or "Sea-Glass-Jewelry."

Once your title has been accepted, click "Next" and you will be asked to enter tags. If you're stuck for inspiration, choose three of the main tags you use for your Etsy items.

For my example, I would use:

The best tag for my lens is: Sea Glass Jewelry

3 more good ones are: Beach Glass, Natural Jewelry, Beach Jewelry

It's worth mentioning at this point that if you have a number of different items in your Etsy shop, for instance, sea glass necklaces, sea glass earrings, et cetera, you can always set up a lens for each. The more lenses you create, the more potential exposure you will receive from both Squidoo and the search engines (Squidoo sites rank really well).

The next step will ask you if you wish to do-
nate any earnings to a charity or have them paid to you. Squidoo pages are similar in some regards to sites that use Google AdSense. For example, you may visit a travel Web site and if you click on one of the ads on the Web site the owner gets paid a commission. Whether you donate your proceeds to charity or to your bank account is up to you.

Introduction

The Introduction, Contents & Discovery Tool is a place to introduce people to your lens and give them a taste of the types of things you will cover in your lens. A tip that helps me to write any type of content—from blog posts to articles and copy for sites like Squidoo—is to create a small outline of text ahead of writing. This helps keep my writing focused as well as staying on topic.

Here's an example of how I would set out my introduction:

- An introduction to sea glass and how it is formed
- How I came to create jewelry
- How I discovered Etsy and began selling

Your text should be a decent length, because Squidoo gives you a quality score for your lenses and they want to see a fair amount of content. I would suggest aiming for a minimum of three hundred words for this.

You can also turn your keywords into anchor text, and at the time of writing you can use up to nine links pointing to the same domain. I say "at the time of writing" because Squidoo's terms change from time to time.

The benefit of anchor text is that the search engines can "read" it and the more they see anchor text linked to a Web site the more they will potentially associate the Web site with an "anchored" keyword. If the search engines indexed my Squidoo lens and I have anchored text reading "Sea Glass Jewelry," then this has the potential, coupled with the page rank of Squidoo, for my lens to rank well for the term "Sea Glass Jewelry." Anchor text is a very strong way of creating a link and is well worth learning!

Here's an example of anchor text:

```
<a href="http://www.seaglassjewelrybox
example.etsy.com">Sea Glass Jewelry</a>
```

Once this is saved in Squidoo (or any Web site) it will appear on the page in a blue font that tells people they can click on it, for example: Sea Glass Jewelry. If you clicked on this link online, you'd be taken straight to my Etsy shop.

You will want to substitute for "seaglassjewelry" the name of your Etsy shop and then place your keyword where I have ">Sea Glass Jewelry</a>." For example:

```
<a href="http://www.[your Etsyshop].etsy.
com">[your keyword]</a>.
```

To further emphasize your anchor text, you could use bold, underline, and italic. Here's the code you need for **bold**:

```
<a href="http://www.[yourEtsyshop].etsy.com">
<b>your keyword<b></a>
```

Italics:

```
<a href="http://www.[yourEtsyshop].etsy.com">
<i>[your keyword]<i></a>
```

<u>Underlined:</u>

```
<a href="http://www.[yourEtsyshop].etsy.com">
<u>[your keyword]<u></a>
```

If you're new to anchor text and HTML code, the above may look a little intimidating, but once you try it for yourself you'll see how simple it is. You can experiment within your Squidoo lens, and as soon as you get the hang of creating anchor text you can use it on any Web site that allows it (your blog will be a great place for anchor text!).

You can also add an image to spice up your introduction. I recommend using a different image for your bio picture and would certainly make it one of my best Etsy items, something that would make people want to learn more about me.

As well as your intro text there's also a tab for "Table of Contents"—which you can switch on to make your lens more reader friendly. Squidoo points out that using this can increase readership and potentially gather more clicks on ads.

Finally, there's a Discovery Tool, and this is a great way to increase visitors by suggesting three other lenses that are related to yours. The lens-masters whom you link to, and who are participating with the Discovery Tool, can then send traffic back to you.

Text

You can use the "New Text" module to add more content to your lens or continue on from the copy you created in your introduction module.

Again, you should aim to make your content a few paragraphs and also include your keywords, but be careful not to overuse them, as this can lead your content to look "spammy" and may appear awkward for the reader.

When you open up your text module (by clicking on "Edit") you'll need to give it a title and try to use your keyword within a natural context.

I recommend deciding what this text module is going to be about before you start writing so that you can avoid writer's block. Perhaps you could write about a few techniques you use in your work or share some useful tips you've found or give a brief history of your craft.

So for my Sea Glass Jewelry lens, I would use the following in the **Text module**:

Give your module a title: Sea Glass Jewelry Designs

Give your module a subtitle: Natural Jewelry on Etsy

Enter your text below: This is where you will want to add a description of why you love creating and crafting. You can also use anchor text here. For instance:

<a href="http://www.etsy.com/shop/SeaGlassJewelryBoxExample">Sea Glass Jewelry</a>

You can also add photographs of your work to break up your text and to make your module look more compelling.

As mentioned, Squidoo monitors the amount of outbound links and the level of self promotion in their Lenses. So to avoid your Lens being "Locked" and subject to review, I would use anchor text sparingly. It's also best to consider the reader as well, as reading overly self-promotional copy can sometimes be a turn off.

You can use the HTML prompts I discussed earlier to bold, underline, and italicize your text, so if you wanted to highlight a couple of your keywords in the text module, all you have to do is include a "<b>" for bold, "<i>" to italicize, or "<u>" to underline. For example, "<b>keyword<b>" will make the text keyword **bold**.

Modules

A module is a section you choose to add and populate with content. For example, you can choose a video module to share YouTube videos with. You can add as many modules as you like to Squidoo, and it is worth fully exploring the site to find ways of improving your lens and giving value to the reader. To add a module, visit the right-hand side of the screen as shown below. I recommend at least adding the following three modules:

GUESTBOOK

Having a Guestbook on your lens means that people can leave comments at the foot of your page. This is a great way to interact with people and make new contacts and therefore potential customers. When you first create your lens it may take some time for your Guestbook to receive entries, so you could always direct friends, family, or contacts on Etsy, Twitter, and Facebook to leave comments and get the ball rolling.

You can "edit" your Guestbook and any module whenever you choose using the "Edit" button:

I would leave the Guestbook options at the default settings, which allow anyone to post to your Guestbook as well as requesting for you to approve comments (you'll be notified by e-mail). This can help to ensure you maintain the quality of comments left on your Guestbook. You can also change the title of your Guestbook module, which defaults to "Guestbook." I changed mine to "Sea Glass Jewelry Guestbook" in keeping with the titles of my other modules.

RSS

RSS allows you to receive automatic updates as soon as your favorite Web sites update their content. This is an excellent way of staying up-to-date and can save you lots of time. I have my Google Reader set up on my personal account to monitor a variety of Web sites for new stories. I hope you have already set up a Google Reader linked with your

"Etsy Gmail" account (as covered in the Twitter chapter) and have begun receiving updates. The RSS module in your Squidoo lens acts in the same manner and will pull in updates from your Etsy shop (or Web site).

To add your Etsy shop feed, visit your Etsy shop's front page, scroll down to "Actions," and right-click on "Subscribe to feed," copy the link location, and paste it into your RSS module back on the Squidoo site.

Example settings I would use for my RSS Feed Modules are:

Give your module a title: Sea Glass Jewelry Designs

Give your module a description: New Sea Glass Jewelry Designs and Organic, Natural Jewelry on Etsy

RSS FEED DETAILS

What URL would you like to pull your RSS from?

http://youretsyshoprssfeed (you need to copy and paste this from your Etsy shop: Subscribe to Feed")

How many headlines would you like to show?

I would choose three headlines, which will keep your page from being cluttered. This will give people an opportunity to see the titles of your listings and, if you've given your items appealing titles, this can be a further chance to bring shoppers to your Etsy store.

Would you like to include an exerpt from each link in the feed? —Excerpt 100 characters

How frequently should the module be updated? —1 day

Would you like to display HTML in the excerpt —Yes

Finally, click "Save," and your Etsy feed should now be showing on your Squidoo lens. One caveat is that if you have too many outbound links to Etsy in your lens you may need to change this feed. You will discover if you have too many links to Etsy when you come to publish your Squidoo lens and receive a warning that it cannot be published until edited. If you have too many links to Etsy, you can use your blogs' RSS feed.

VIDEO MODULE

Click "Edit" on your video module to give it a new title:

Give your module a title: Sea Glass Jewelry Videos

Give your module a description: A showcase of fresh and innovative Sea

Glass Jewelry designs on Etsy

Paste the video link here: As instructed, this is where you paste the links to the videos you want to share on your Squidoo Lens.

To find videos to post that relate to your niche, you can visit YouTube or other video-sharing sites such as Metacafe or Vimeo or simply type in "List of video hosting websites" into Wikipedia:

en.wikipedia.org/wiki/Main_Page

Once you have found a video-hosting site, type in a relevant keyword or keywords ("Sea Glass Jewelry" for example) to find content to share on your Squidoo lens.

You can add as many video modules as you like, so if you have a series of videos that you wish to share, simply add new modules. The videos you choose can be anything you think will be of interest to people visiting your lens. Later in the book you're going to learn how to create your own YouTube videos in Chapter 32, so you can always come back to your lens and copy and paste the URLs from your own YouTube videos.

ETSY MODULE

As well as the three modules that you can include from the "Add Modules" shortcut, you can also add an Etsy module. To do this go to the "Add Modules" shortcut on the right-hand-side menu and at the bottom of the box click on "Browse all modules." You will then be taken to another page where you can run a search for modules, simply type in "Etsy" and "Go," and click the + sign to add the Etsy module and then "Done Adding."

You'll need to click on "Edit" on your Etsy module to give it a title, subtitle (if you choose), and brief description before clicking "Add Items."

On the next screen type in your Etsy shop name and click on "Search" and, once your items are showing, click "Save."

Other modules that are worth adding are "Flickr" and "Twitter Follow," and you can add both of these using the method shown above.

There are plenty of different modules to experiment with and choose from, and it's worth browsing through the various options until you get your lens looking the way you want it. You can also reorder your modules using the boxes underneath "Add Modules" by dragging them up and down.

Once you've finished with your Squidoo lens, click on "Publish" at the top of the page. If there are any issues with your lens you will get a warning. Common problems that occur can be not enough text or content or too many instances of anchor text. If this is the case, simply follow the instructions to edit your lens, and once you have completed the requested changes your lens will be published.

When your lens is live on Squidoo, copy your lens's URL and you can then Stumble it, add it to Facebook and Twitter, and get the word out!

ACTION STEPS

- ☐ Sign up for a Squidoo account.
- ☐ Write an introduction for your Squidoo lens, including anchor text.
- ☐ Create a text module with written content.
- ☐ Add Guestbook, RSS, video, and Etsy modules to your lens.
- ☐ Make a note to return and add your YouTube video after it's been created.

Your HubPage

28

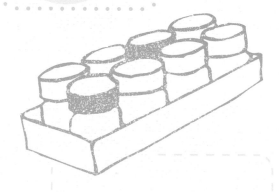

HUBPAGES, like Squidoo, is a Web 2.0 site that allows you to create your own content and share it with a thriving community. The sky is the limit with HubPages, and if you can think of a topic there's a chance someone has created a HubPage about it, and if they haven't you could be the first! Not only can you market your work, but if someone clicks on one of the advertisements on your HubPage you may also get paid!

HubPages is also an excellent way to promote your business, and creating a link to your Etsy shop or blog has a further benefit: HubPages rank incredibly well with the search engines.

To set up your first HubPage, visit:

hubpages.com/signin/

First, click on the "sign up now" option. You'll find a fairly standard sign-up form, but when it comes to choosing your HubPages, name you'll need to choose wisely, as this cannot be changed at a later date. For my example I'd choose my username as "Sea Glass Jewelry." Your username may already be taken, so you may need to be a little creative; however, using your keyword is a really good idea where possible.

For e-mail address I'd recommend using the e-mail linked to your Etsy shop, which helps to keep everything in the same place and therefore easier to find. You will have to choose a password, agree to HubPages' terms, and enter a CAPT-CHA before clicking on "Create My Account."

The next page will ask you to provide a little bit of information, including your hobbies and interests, and while you can skip this step if you choose, it's worth taking the time to fill this out to create a more rounded profile. For my example I'd add:

Sea Glass Jewelry, Etsy, Arts and Crafts

The page will then expand and HubPages will suggest further topics that may be of interest and which you can choose if you feel they are relevant.

Once you've completed this exercise, you'll be asked if you want to search through your e-mail contacts for friends and contacts who may also be signed up for HubPages. This is entirely up to you; however, if you've only just signed up for your new Gmail account while reading this book, you may want to skip this step.

On the next page, click on the large button "Create A Hub."

Title

The first option is to create a title for your Hub. In order to gain the most exposure, enter your keyword/Etsy shop name. If your keyword has already been taken by someone else, then you'll need to adjust your Hub's unique address in the box below. A simple way to do this is by adding a word (or suffix) at the end of your keyword.

At the time of writing, "Sea Glass Jewelry" is available, but if it wasn't, I'd add "blog" at the end of my Web address as highlighted below:

Create A Hub
Simplified Version

1 **Choose a Title**

Sea Glass Jewelry

2 **Give Your Hub a Unique Web Address**

Sea-Glass-Jewelry-blog

http://www.hubpages.com/hub/Sea-Glass-Jewelry-blog

The next box requires you to give your Hub a topic. I chose "Arts and Design," as this is a perfect choice for an Etsy shop, and from there you can keep using the drop-down option until you find a category that accurately describes your shop:

Arts and Design → Crafts & Handiwork → Jewelry Making

In the next box you're given the option to choose a layout for your HubPage, which I leave at the default, but you may wish to experiment.

Finally, you need to add two tags, and these should be your main keyword plus one other tag that sums up your line of business. For this example I'd choose "sea glass jewelry" and "beach jewelry" before clicking on "Continue."

Warning

On the next screen you receive a warning from HubPages about posting "spam, copied & inappropriate content," and it's well worth clicking on "Learn More." This will help you to familiarize yourself with the activities that are banned on HubPages, in order to avoid being penalized. As well as "Adult," "Gambling," and "Spam" you may notice that HubPages also disallow pages that are "Low Quality." This essentially means they do not want people putting up pages with the minimum amount of work just to get a quick backlink, as this is of low value to HubPages visitors.

You should ensure you create all-new content for your HubPage. You've already created similar content in your Squidoo lens, but please ensure that the copy you add to HubPages is entirely different. You could use some of the material you wrote earlier as the basis for new content; however, it will need to be thoroughly rewritten and reworked so that it's completely unique.

Once you've read through HubPages' terms, click "Continue," enter the CAPTCHA, and "Continue."

In Squidoo, your content was arranged in modules, which correspond to HubPages' capsules, so you should already be familiar with the concept. The first thing I would add is a photograph to liven up the page. You can do this by clicking on the "photo" capsule and then "edit":

You will then be given the opportunity to give your capsule a subtitle, choose a picture, and upload it from your computer. You may notice that I have changed my capsule subtitle from "Sea Glass Jewelry" to "Beach Jewelry" to avoid being repetitive. As mentioned previously, you need to balance optimizing your Web 2.0 sites for both the search engines and readers.

Click "save" at the top of the capsule when you wish to upload, and depending on the size of your image and the speed of your connection, this may take some time.

You can also add another "photo" capsule in addition to the current one. Including as much content as possible is going to increase your chances of having your HubPage published and you also get to show off more of your work, which is a win-win situation!

To add more capsules, go to the right-hand side of the page and click on the boxes illustrated below. As well as photos, I've also highlighted three other capsules that I recommend using:

You can now add more images to your Hub-Page, so you will want to choose some of your best items to feature and when you upload them add brief descriptions for each.

Text

The next capsule to populate is going to be the text capsule. Again, click "edit" to open the box and begin typing. While there is no minimal length for your text, bear in mind that HubPages score you on the amount of content you add, so, as with Squidoo, I'd look to make my article/copy a minimum of two to three hundred words. You can also bold or italicize words to break your copy up and help people who scan-read to find relevant information.

To make your anchor text, simply highlight the word/s you wish to use and then click on the "link" symbol:

When you're finished, click on "save" and your copy should appear on your HubPage. This is a great opportunity to preview your text and edit before your HubPage is published.

Comments

The next capsule is comments, and this is definitely worth including on your HubPage, as it's where people can interact with you and share their own interests and experiences. For the capsule subtitle, I have asked a question in the hope that it will provoke a response and encourage people to comment:

> Do you have a passion for Sea Glass Jewelry? Share your comments here!

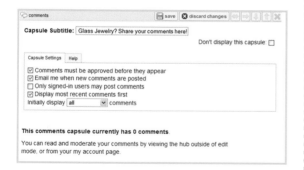

I've also marked the option for comments to be approved by me before they are posted and requested an e-mail alert when new comments are posted. I have set the option so that the most recent comments are posted first, which will help your HubPage look up-to-date.

Videos

You can also add videos to your HubPage. For now you may like to add videos from YouTube, although later in the book you'll learn how to make your own videos and so it's worth returning to this chapter and section at a later stage.

For now simply go to YouTube (or another video-sharing Web site such as blip.tv, Google, Metacafe, Revver, Vimeo, and Yahoo! Video) and find a video that ties in with your work. You'll need to copy the video's URL and paste it into your HubPages video capsule.

This is a really quick and simple way of adding fresh and interesting content to your Hub and, I hope, enticing visitors to stay on your page.

Links

The links capsule is really straightforward. Click "edit" and then you can add a link to your Hub-Page. You can try your Etsy shop, but if there are too many instances of your Etsy URL on your Hub you may be told to change this when it comes to publishing, so instead you could add your blog, Twitter, or Facebook Page.

You can also give your links capsule a title, for example:

Capsule Subtitle: Sea Glass Jewelry Resources
Add Links by: URL
URL: http://YOURWEBSITE.com

RSS

Your RSS capsule is very straightforward and you could add the feed from your Etsy shop, or if that URL is overused on your HubPage, add your blog feed. You can add an RSS feed from anywhere on the Internet that has RSS capabilities.

Adding this capsule can help your HubPage to carry brand-new content without having to manually add it yourself, because once you have added your feed it updates itself as soon as fresh content appears via the source you included. For example, if you add your Etsy shop's feed and then list new items, they will also appear in the RSS capsule on your HubPage.

Tags

You should try to make sure you add as many tags as possible to your HubPage so that people searching can find you. This is the same exercise as when you tag your Etsy items. HubPages will also suggest additional tags for you. Using the illustration, I'd select "glass jewelry," "sea glass," and "Etsy," as these are all valid for my page. To get more ideas, check through your Etsy listings and add in relevant tags.

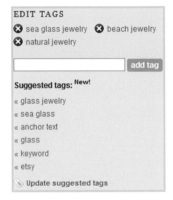

It's worth looking through the other capsule options to see if there are any other options that you may wish to include on your page. Adding a "quiz" and "poll" are certainly two ways to provide your visitors with a more interactive experience.

You can also "reorder" your capsules and re-build your page the way you want it:

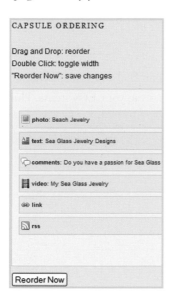

The way it's currently set works in terms of attracting people with an image and then following up with your all-important text module, but you may prefer to change your setup.

Profile

Finally, I suggest you make some changes to your profile to personalize your HubPage. To do this, head to "My Profile" in the top right-hand menu and then "Edit Profile."

The first choice is to "Add a Photo." You can either choose a photograph of yourself (which is a great way to inspire trust in visitors) or, if you prefer, upload a picture of one of your creations. On the next screen you'll need to upload your picture. You will then be given a chance to crop it so that it fits on HubPages by repositioning the square to frame your picture and then clicking "Crop the Image."

You can also add your location (town or city is fine for this exercise) and choose how you want to be contacted by HubPages (if at all).

On the right-hand side of the page is a box for your bio, where you can add some brief text as a short summary for readers. Try to ensure that you include your keyword in this space (which you can also bold); you can also add a link and make it anchor text by highlighting your text and clicking on the "link" symbol and adding your URL.

You also get an option to include your actual name and address, but personally I skip this step.

Publish!

Once you're finished, you can click "Preview" to check over the layout of your HubPage and, when you're satisfied, click on "Publish Now."

Once your HubPage is published, copy the URL and socially bookmark it with Su.pr, Twitter, and Facebook and add it to your blog or Web site.

You have now added content on the Internet and gained two advantages: first, the visitors to

HubPages who are searching for content that ties in with your keyword may become potential customers and, second, you're getting a powerful backlink to your Etsy shop and blog from a Web site that ranks incredibly well with the search engines.

ACTION STEPS

- Sign up for a HubPages account.
- Add plenty of images to your HubPage.
- Add video, photos, links, and RSS capsules.
- Write a new article for your text module.
- Make a note to return and post your YouTube video once it has been created.
- Publish your HubPage.
- Find other Hubs of interest and leave supportive comments and feedback in their Guestbooks.

Further Web 2.0 Sites

29

SO FAR we've looked at a number of Web 2.0 sites where you can add a profile, share links to your Web site and Etsy shop, and interact with other users. There are other Web sites where you can create a profile, and they have the same advantage as Facebook, Twitter, HubPages, and Squidoo (i.e., further exposure to users and invaluable backlinks to your Etsy shop or blog). These links are often incredibly powerful, as a number of these sites experience a high ranking within the search engines, partly due to the sheer amount of fresh and quality content that is posted to them daily. Another factor is the high amount of traffic they receive; both of these traits are common with Web 2.0 sites.

Other sites that are worth setting up a profile with follow.

Tumblr

www.tumblr.com/

Tumblr is very similar to both HubPages and Squidoo; you build your own page using your own content, and once you've set up your profile you can follow other people with their own Tumblr pages. This is similar to Twitter: strengthening and building a supportive network of people with similar interests to your own. You also have a wealth of themes to choose from and can customize your own, as well as connecting your Tumblr page with Facebook.

Tumblr has a huge community and it's a fantastic place to showcase your Etsy creations.

Weebly

Weebly is another Web 2.0 site where you can quickly and simply build your own Web site and blog with a minimal learning curve while using an incredibly intuitive drag and drop interface. You can make your Weebly page stand out with a host of professionally designed themes, and it's completely free to use. This site also carries a page rank of 8/10 with Google, which makes it a powerful place from which to receive a backlink.

Posterous

Unlike a lot of Web sites, Posterous is uncluttered and extremely straightforward. When you find a Web page that you like and wish to share, you simply send an e-mail to Posterous and they upload the content to your own unique page. You can also include photographs along with your text, as well as sharing videos. Another great feature is that Posterous can act as a hub; each time you make a post, your content can be sent automatically to your other Web 2.0 sites, including Facebook, Twitter, Flickr, Tumblr, and Word-Press.

Posterous is a great way to feed other content and distribute it through your Web 2.0 network, and this content could be fun items you find on Google Reader and simply wish to share with your audience quickly and simply without having to write text. Within Google Reader's settings is an option to post directly to your Posterous page, which can save you a lot of time and effort!

Myspace

Myspace is one of the original sites that allowed people to create their own profiles and share content with other users. A common perception is that people have moved to Facebook from Myspace, but there is still a huge amount of Myspace users and they constitute an entirely different demographic than Facebook. If you wish to reach as wide an audience as possible, then it's definitely worth taking some time to establish a presence with Myspace.

Yahoo! Answers

Yahoo! Answers is a wonderful place to connect with other people as well as help others and, at the same time, build yourself as an authority within your niche. As an artist or crafter you will be familiar with a wide range of topics that relate to your work, and if you find people asking related questions you should be able to answer quickly and simply. Yahoo! Answers ranks really well with the search engines and provides a powerful backlink. The only thing to be careful of is that you do not continuously answer people's questions with a link to your shop, as this will be flagged as spam and your account may be closed. The best way to use Yahoo! Answers to raise awareness of your Etsy shop is by being courteous and helpful, which will then, I hope, lead people to click on your profile to learn more about you.

deviantART

The deviantART site is an excellent place for creative people to share their work and is a well-known showcase for visual arts including painting, illustrations, and photography. There is a wide and varied audience within deviantART, who form a vibrant online community of artists. Apart from uploading your work to your own page, you can join groups of like-minded artists and many will give you feedback on your work. Whatever niche you're in, be it jewelry, art, or sock puppets, run a search on deviantART and if you find an audience, add your own page. If not, you can always start your own!

Which Sites to Post to?

With the sheer wealth of options with Web 2.0 sites you may feel overwhelmed, so it's worth establishing a presence on each, one at a time. One thing to watch for is that your content is not duplicated across these sites and that it remains fully original.

When it comes to finding new information or content to share with your audience, you could use Google Reader and alerts to get new ideas.

So which site do you post to? Primarily I recommend posting to your blog and then alerting your Twitter and Facebook audiences to your new content using Su.pr. With the sites mentioned in this chapter, as long as you can include an RSS feed from your blog they will be automatically updated as and when you post new content on your blog.

ACTION STEPS

- ☐ Sign up for a Tumblr account.
- ☐ Create a Weebly account.
- ☐ Register with Posterous.
- ☐ Join Myspace.
- ☐ Sign up for a Yahoo! Answers account.
- ☐ Explore and join deviantART.

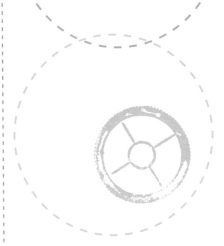

Writing a Mini-masterpiece with EzineArticles

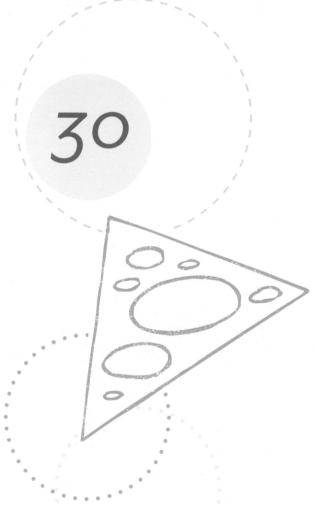

30

ARTICLE MARKETING is a favorite technique with Internet marketers who are looking to get exposure within a host of different niches, and there is absolutely no reason why you can't apply this technique to your Etsy shop. The Internet is mainly made up of information; it's like a huge magazine with masses of articles and features, columns and diaries. Web sites are constantly looking out for new material and will often turn to article directories for fresh content to post to their site. An article directory is a place where you can post your articles for other people to use on their Web sites and, in return, you receive a backlink to your site as well as exposure. If a Web site uses your article, they will be required to include your "author's resource box," which is an area where you include a link back to your Web site. Therefore, ensuring you write a relevant and well-written article increases your chances of it being picked up by other Web sites, which is an excellent way of receiving free viral marketing and appearing as an authority within your niche.

EzineArticles

EzineArticles is the number one place to post when it comes to article directories, and your blog will receive a powerful backlink when you publish. Ezine is also one of the first places that Web site owners turn to when they need relevant content, so there's high potential for receiving a diverse amount of visitors back to your site.

The idea of writing articles might be a little intimidating at first, but it's really very simple and once you turn in a couple of articles and get them accepted for publication it can be incredibly fulfilling. You don't need to worry about writing masses of content, either, but each article does need to be a minimum of 400 words and shouldn't exceed 5,000. If you have a particularly long article, then you could always break it down into a series of articles.

Before you get started, you should read the terms of service for EzineArticles; they are brief and easy to follow and could be the difference between you getting your article published or rejected:

ezinearticles.com/author-terms-of-service.html

ezinearticles.com/editorial-guidelines.html

Originality

As with Squidoo and HubPages, the content you write needs to be 100 percent original. You could take some of your earlier writing, break it up, and paraphrase it if you're stuck for ideas, but the article will have to pass the duplicate content test, so it's no good copying and pasting existing content.

To set up an account with EzineArticles, head to:

ezinearticles.com/submit/

You will need to fill in all of the contact details and account information and make sure you also include the URL for your blog or Web site. I recommend that whenever you have to submit your URL, you actually visit your Web site, highlight the URL in your browser, and right-click and copy and then paste it rather than typing it in from memory. This can avoid unnecessary typos and errors.

Once you have finished with the signing-up process, click on "Create My Account!"

You may be required to confirm your account by e-mail, so log in to the e-mail address you provided in the setup and follow the instructions to verify your account.

Submitting

Once you've verified your account, sign in and go to "Article Manager" in the top left-hand side of the screen and click on "Submit new article."

First, you need to give your article a category, and it's worth taking some time to go through the options and select a category that fits your article. This is important, as the easier you make it for people to find your writing, the more likely it will be read and published.

For my example I would choose the following options:

Select a category: Shopping-and-Product-Reviews

Subcategory: Jewelry—Diamonds

After you've selected your category, you will be asked to enter a title for your article, and this is important because you'll need to use your keyword and work it into your title in some way. You will need to construct your headline in a way that flows naturally to both the reader and editors at EzineArticles.

It's important to note that before your article is published and goes live on EzineArticles, it needs to pass an evaluation by at least one editor. Ezine can be pretty strict, which is understandable, as they only want to publish quality content for their readers. To allow for this, you should take care to write an article that gives the reader information of value, as well as, I hope, ranking well for your keyword.

Sometimes my articles have been rejected by an editor, but if this happens to you, don't worry, because it happens! You can appeal decisions, and by keeping within the guidelines you will lessen the chances of being rejected. Essentially, make sure your article isn't an advertisement for your shop—that's what the resource box is for at the end of your article (more on this in a moment).

It's good to start your title with your keyword phrase. An easy and popular way to write your article is by using lists and numbers, for example, "Sea Glass Jewelry - Three ways to preserve it."

For people who are in a hurry, reading an article with a numbered list helps with skim reading. They can absorb the main points simply and quickly without having to read the whole article. By using the number of facts within the title you can also help people get an instant idea of the key facts they're going to learn by reading your article.

If you're stuck for ideas, enter your keyword into the Internet and skim through results until you find some interesting facts. You could also use Google Reader to find a number of ideas for articles. Clearly, you can't just copy information, but you can certainly find material that will form a good base for an article. Yahoo! Answers often has a lot of good information, and you could also use EzineArticles for further ideas. Sometimes one simple sentence can act as a springboard for an article.

For instance: SeaGlassJewelry—Three ways to preserve it.

After your title, you need to include a summary of your article. Once you've written your article, you will probably want to come back to this box and summarize your content in a couple of sentences that will make people want to read on. Think of this as a teaser; for example:

> Learn essential ways to protect and store your Sea Glass from wear and tear and other harmful elements. Beach glass is an absolutely beautiful gift from Mother Nature, but it's also an incredibly delicate material—here's three quick and simple tips to protect your jewelry and ensure its longevity while keeping it clean and safe.

Text Editors

You may find it easy to write your article in a Word document or some other form of word-processing software before you copy and paste it into EzineArticles. This can help if you don't want to have to write your whole article in one sitting. A further benefit is, if your Internet connection is broken for any reason, you won't lose your work.

If you use word-processing software, you can sometimes end up with strange formatting issues when you paste your text into a site like Ezine-Articles, so you need to strip out the formatting. This is done easily by pasting your text into a free piece of software such as Windows Notepad (or TextEdit for Macs) to remove the formatting, before copying and pasting from your notepad into EzineArticles.

Main Article

So now it's time to enter your main article, and whether you have written it already or prefer to write it live in EzineArticles, your text needs to go in the "Article Body" box.

You really don't need to write an epic and should try to have fun with your article, rather than treating it as you would a school assignment (which for many people wasn't too much fun).

While you want your article to be grammatically correct, keeping things loose and conversational is a great way to write online content. If you approach your article in the same way you would write to a friend, this can come across to the reader and make your work accessible and light.

As mentioned, people like to see bullet points or numbered lists, and using the WYSIWYG editor allows this:

"WYSIWYG" stands for "What You See Is What You Get" and is a simple editor that allows you to format your text. One of the available options is bullet points, so if you have a few points that you wish to make with your article, using the "Bullet Point" option can break up your text and make it stand out for people who skim-read:

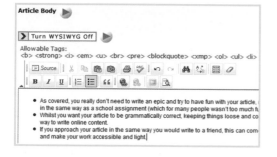

You can also bold, italicize, and underline your keywords, although I recommend using this in no more than three instances throughout your text and only once per one hundred words.

Another way to make your article accessible to the reader, and this goes for most text, is to use plenty of paragraphs. When you're reading text online and in magazines you may notice a lot of writers employ this technique. Even though you're getting the same information, having plenty of spaces makes it look far less intimidating than huge blocks of text.

A good way to see how to format your articles is by browsing through existing articles on Ezine. Search for topics of interest and look at a few examples to get some illustrations of formatting. You may even pick up some more ideas for your own article; perhaps the author missed out some key points that occur to you.

Below your article is a small box that lets you know how many words you've written; this is really handy and helps ensure you cover the minimum amount of 400 words. There's no firm rule of thumb with the length of your article (aside from the minimum and maximum word count), but usually the more information and content the better. The more quality information you share with your audience and the more you can establish yourself as an authority, the higher the chances that readers will click on the link you leave in your resource box at the foot of the article.

Keywords

Below your author's box is a space to include keywords, and by now this should be a very familiar exercise. You need to ensure your keywords are relevant to your article and use commas between each keyword, using a minimum of four or five.

Author's Resource Box

Once you've completed your article, you have the opportunity to include information about yourself, and this needs to be written in a way that will make people want to click on your link to learn more. Writing this bio in the third person is a common technique.

Try to ensure this information is brief and to the point. You will also need to include a "call to action," i.e., text that acts as a command and tells people what to do next.

Again, you should use anchor text to get the most out of this exercise:

```
<a href="http://www.[yourwebsite].com">
[your keyword]</a>
```

Here's an example of a resource box:

> Derrick Sutton is an artist, writer, and
> <a href="http://www.seaglassjewelryblog">
> Sea Glass Jewelry</a> designer.
> You can find a wealth of information by visiting
> his <a href="http://www.seaglassjewelryblog">
> Sea Glass Jewelry</a> Web site.

Preview and Submit

Before you submit your article, click "Preview article" to ensure you're happy with the formatting and content and ensure that the links you included in your resource box work (you can click on them and they should take you to your Web site).

Once you've finished, it's time to click on "Submit this article" and agree to the terms and conditions.

Approval and publication of your article can take over a week, depending on the volume of articles being submitted. You can see the progress of your submission by logging in and clicking on "Article Manager" and "Pending Articles."

You will receive e-mailed updates as your article passes through the various stages of publication. If it is rejected, try not to get disheartened. Instead, make the suggested changes and resubmit. If you don't believe that the rejection is justified, then you can contact EzineArticles and explain your reasons, although it's best to be a hundred percent sure of your facts before contacting them.

Once your article is live and published, make sure you socially bookmark it in all the usual places!

One final point is not to stop with the one article; you can write as many as you like, and the more you publish the more exposure you receive online, plus the more high-value backlinks you gain pointing back to your Web site.

A C T I O N   S T E P S

- ◌ Sign up for an EzineArticles account.
- ◌ Write your first keyword-optimized article.
- ◌ Create a compelling call to action within your resource box, including anchor text and a link back to your Web site.
- ◌ Make a note to check back on the progress of your article's publication.
- ◌ Fix any suggested changes from EzineArticles' editors if your article is rejected.
- ◌ Stumble your published article and post its URL to Twitter, Facebook, and other Web 2.0 sites.

Advertising with craigslist

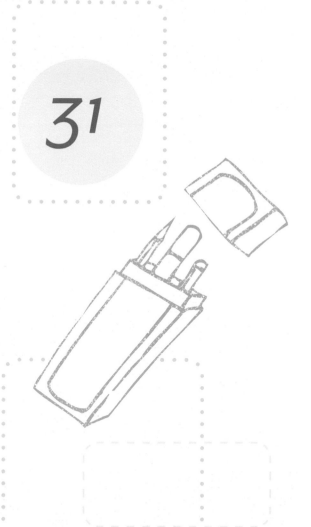

31

THE FREE ONLINE CLASSIFIEDS

Web site craigslist is an excellent place for you to get the word out about your Etsy shop.

For anyone who isn't familiar with craigslist, it's a wonderful resource where you can find all sorts of items and services, from personals to housing, items for sale to jobs, but for the purpose of this exercise we will be using craigslist to advertise your Etsy items.

The craigslist site has a few rules that you need to observe, and it's definitely worth reading through these terms to avoid your advertisement being "flagged." Like a lot of Web sites, craigslist has a large community, which is often "self-policed," meaning if someone spots something that they consider inappropriate or against craigslist terms they will flag it for removal.

You can post an advertisement for your Etsy shop and creations in the "for sale" section and you could also add a profile page about yourself in the "artists" section under "community"; just be sure that you're not selling specific items in both advertisements, as this would count as duplicate posting and may get you flagged.

To post an ad on craigslist, visit:

http://www.craigslist.org/about/sites

Before you post, familiarize yourself with craigslist's terms and conditions to avoid being flagged and having your ad removed. The terms can be found on the left-hand side of the page under "terms of use."

Next you need to choose your city or nearest area or state. It's vital that you choose the most relevant location to you, as this is a strict rule on craigslist and failing to do so could lead your ad to being flagged.

Once you're ready to post your advertisement, simply click on "post to classifieds."

The best option in the following selection is "for sale," and for my sample Etsy shop the next option would be "arts & crafts."

When you post an ad, the first section you need to fill in is the title for your item. This title needs to be as accurate as possible, not only to aid people searching but also to avoid your ad being flagged.

You'll now need to enter text for the main body of your advertisement. The best way to write ad copy for craigslist is by being both friendly and professional, as well as making your advertisement as compelling as possible. You may wish to reread "Writing Listings That Sell" for more ideas. There really is no difference between the text you write for craigslist and the writing you use in your Etsy listings; essentially, you need to sell!

You can also include anchor text to create a clickable link to your Etsy shop. Here's an example of text I would use to create my own anchor text:

> This listing is for a beautiful piece of <a href="http://www.etsy.com/shop/SeaGlassJewelryBoxExample">Sea Glass Jewelry</a> that has been fashioned into a necklace.
> The Sea Glass is a gorgeous, subtle shade of blue; a truly one-of-a-kind piece of jewelry.

The above advertisement is brief, as it's merely for example. Points to include in your advertisement would be how the customer will benefit from owning your work and also a strong call to action, i.e., informing the reader where they can find more of your creations (your Etsy shop).

Contact

Above your main advert are two options that are set by default to "anonymize" (they will show as: "sale-xxxxxxx@craigslist.org"); you can either choose the default or allow people to contact you at your e-mail address. My personal preference is to leave this at the default and keep my anonymity.

Below your advertisement is a place where you can upload four images; again, you will want to make sure that these are your strongest images.

You can test to see how your advertisement will appear at any time by clicking "Continue," which will then give you a preview, and at any point you can go back and make changes by clicking on "Edit."

Once your advertisement is ready, you will need to click "Continue" once more and agree to craigslist's terms of use before verifying your listing by e-mail.

Providing your advertisement isn't flagged for any reason, it will be live for a week and you can then repost it, although it's important to note that you cannot have two identical ads running at the same time.

I would suggest you add your craigslist listings to your calendar so you can see when they're going to expire and ensure you repost and maintain your presence on craigslist.

As well as making sales via craigslist, you may find you are contacted by people at shops within your area who are looking to stock the types of items you make. By constructing a really well-written advertisement you can open up a whole new vista of possibilities for your work, and it doesn't cost you a penny!

ACTION STEPS

- Familiarize yourself with craiglist's terms and conditions.
- Write and publish an advertisement using anchor text.
- Note when your advertisement is going to expire in your calendar and repost (taking care not to have two duplicate advertisements running).

Make a Movie with YouTube

32

YOUTUBE is growing at an amazing rate and it's actually catching up with the likes of Google, Yahoo!, and Bing as a search engine in its own right.

Google owns YouTube, which means you will need to use your Google account once again! This is a really worthwhile exercise, because by sharing your Etsy items on YouTube you reach a new range of people who use YouTube as a search engine over the more traditional sites. Some of the people searching on YouTube may not have heard of Etsy, so you could be introducing a whole new audience to your shop!

This chapter is going to show you how to create your very own video without the use of a video camera, upload it to YouTube, provide it with a soundtrack, and ensure it's fully optimized for the search engines.

Picasa

In order to make your video you will need to download free software called Picasa, which you can download for your PC from:

www.picasaweb.google.com/

Or if you have a Mac:

picasa.google.com/mac/

When you first download and install Picasa, it may ask you if you wish it to scan your entire computer or just your pictures folder in order to find available images to use. This is entirely up to you.

Once Picasa has finished its initial scan, I recommend sorting through and removing any folders or images to which you do not want to grant access. This is important because one of the benefits of Picasa is the ability to share items online; however, there may be personal and private documents and images that you do not wish to upload or make available online.

You can remove folders by selecting the folder within Picasa's interface and then right-clicking your mouse and selecting "Remove from Picasa."

It's important that you select "Remove from Picasa" and not "Delete folder," which could delete the folder from your computer.

You can also control the access that Picasa has to your folders and hard drive by selecting "Tools" from the top menu and then "Folder Manager."

This gives you the options of both allowing and disallowing access to files and folders as you choose.

I recommend you create a new folder on your hard drive especially for this exercise; it will make locating and uploading images a lot easier. Once you have created your new folder, sort through your Etsy listing photographs and select your best images. You should choose at least ten to make a video with a decent length. Copy these images into your Etsy folder and these will be used in your first movie.

You will then need to add this folder to Picasa by visiting the Picasa interface, clicking on "File," then "Add Folder to Picasa," locating the new Etsy folder on your hard drive, and then selecting "Scan once." Now your Etsy images will be added to Picasa.

For this example I've chosen a few photographs I took on the beach, plus one of a piece of sea glass jewelry. If I had an actual Etsy shop with items for sale, I would upload items from my shop, and I recommend you do the same.

Creating Your Movie

To select the photographs I want to use in my video, I simply highlight them in Picasa by either clicking on one at a time to select or pressing "Control" and "A" on a PC or "Command" and "A" on a Mac to select all.

When your images are selected, you will see a blue outline as shown above.

Once you've selected the images you wish to use in your video, simply select "Movie" from the foot of the menu:

Picasa's Movie Suite will now open and it will make a title page from the name of your folder, so you will want to edit this and add the name of your movie instead. You can do this by selecting the "Slide" tab:

Now whatever you type in the box will appear on your title page. You may notice that there are lots of options; you can choose a font, the size and color of the text and background, and where you want your text to be positioned. I recommend "Centered" from the "Template" option to keep your text in the middle of the box.

It's worth experimenting with each of the options until you find one you're happy with. When it comes to the text, you could use the name of your Etsy shop or create a new and compelling title.

Using a bold font can often help make your title stand out, and while white text on a black background may be a little conventional, it works.

At the end of your film you can show another "Title card," which will give viewers the Web address for your Etsy shop. I'll also show you where you can place a clickable link for people to be taken to your Etsy shop or Web site.

Once you've designed your title page, you can rearrange your items by dragging and dropping them:

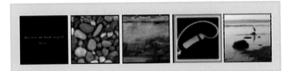

To start off your movie, I'd choose one of your most impressive photographs to act as a "hook" to engage the viewer. For my example I'm only using four photographs, but providing you have a full Etsy shop, you will, I hope, have a lot more to choose from, and the more variety the better, as it can help keep people's interest.

Playback Options

While I recommend including plenty of different pictures, I'd try to keep your film to no more than a couple of minutes.

If you have a few pages of items listed on Etsy and wish to include them all, then it's worth bearing in mind that you can create as many of these videos as you like. Indeed, adding a new one each month is a great way of raising awareness for your Etsy shop.

Another idea is to "theme" your videos, so, for instance, if you had a few items where you use certain colors or materials or have photography based around landscapes or a range of "summer" dresses, you could choose this as your theme.

Going back to your current project, at the top of the interface you may notice the "Movie" tab. Again, take some time to explore the various settings. Here are my preferences:

The reason I selected the Transition Style "Dissolve through black" is because it creates a nice fluid way of moving from one image to another.

You can experiment with the other settings, but one to watch out for is "Slide Duration," which is the length of time an image will appear onscreen. If you have this set too low, then your video will be brief; however, if it's too high you can run the risk of losing people's attention.

Text Slide   (6 of 6)

My personal preference is "Three seconds," as this seems to give the viewer plenty of time to see the item without, I hope, boring them! You can experiment with the various settings and click the green "Play" button below the images to see how your video will appear. This is a good way to get a feel for the correct duration.

Once your images are loaded and you've chosen the running order of your images and transitions and length that each image appears, as well as previewed your video to ensure it's optimized for the viewer, then it's time to put some "End titles" to mark the end of your film.

The caption you use at the end of your film is important and needs to be a call to action for the viewer, an instruction informing them where to go for more details. In this case, I want people to visit my Etsy shop.

To make your caption, click on "Add a new text slide," which can be found under the "Play" button situated just below your video preview screen:

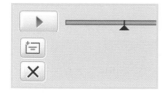

Now drag the new text slide to the end of your film:

You can edit this new text slide the same way you edited the first, and I'd use the same font and sizing and keep it centered. You will want to include the URL of your Etsy shop, and I recommend you visit your shop and copy and paste the URL to avoid any typos.

A further idea is to add another text slide just before your Web address and add some text that will let people know what to do now, such as "To see more Sea Glass Jewelry designs visit…"; then the next slide could be your Web address.

You can add as many text slides as you like and include all sorts of details, but I would try to avoid giving too much information and keep things as simple as possible.

When you paste your final text slide, the end of your film should look something like this:

Now you're finished with your movie, it's time to save it to your hard drive. You can actually upload it directly to YouTube from Picasa, but it's a good idea to have a copy on your hard drive.

To save your film, click on "Create Movie":

You will then see a screen similar to the following illustration. You may need to wait a short time while your film is created by Picasa.

To locate your movie, head back to the main Picasa interface, where you should see a section marked "Movies" and your new film should be showing.

You need to make a note of where your video is stored on your hard drive so that you can upload it

to YouTube. You could also copy or cut the movie from its current location and move it to the folder that contains the photographs you used for your project. To do this, right-click on the movie and select "Locate on Disk." You will then be taken to the folder where the movie is stored and you could copy and paste it into your project folder.

Now you've finished with Picasa, you can close the program.

YouTube

If you already have a YouTube account, unless it's a dedicated account for your Etsy shop I recommend you set up a brand-new account. You can do this by visiting:

www.youtube.com/

At the top right-hand side of the page is the "Create Account" button. Click here and you will be required to register details on the next page. The first question is an important one: your username. I strongly recommend you use either the keyword or keywords that sum up the items you're selling or your Etsy shop name. If either of these options is unavailable, then try a variation. For example, if "Sea Glass Jewelry" was taken, I would try "Sea Glass Jewelry Shop" or "Sea Glass Jewelry Designs."

The rest of the questions are straightforward and you will be required to agree to YouTube's terms and conditions and then click "Create Account."

On the next page, you can either sign up for a new YouTube Google account or sign in with an existing account. I hope by now you have a Gmail account that is dedicated to your Etsy shop, so to save time you can sign in through this account.

You will be asked to verify your e-mail address, so sign into Gmail; just follow the verification instructions.

Once your account is verified, you will be taken back to YouTube. Next, you need to provide some further information to optimize your account. First, click on "Account," which can be reached at any time by clicking on the drop-down menu next to your name and selecting "Account."

My Channel	Subscriptions
Inbox	My Videos
Account	Favorites

The next page shows you an "Overview," which is where you can add or edit information:

| Overview |
| Profile Setup |
| Customize Homepage |
| Playback Setup |
| Email Options |
| Privacy |
| Activity Sharing |
| Mobile Setup |
| Manage Account |

First, click on "Profile Setup," and here you can add a picture (your Etsy avatar, for example), describe yourself using your keyword/Etsy shop name, and add a URL (your Etsy shop).

You can add further details below, including "Personal Details" and "Hometown/Location." Visitors to your page will be able to view this information, which is worth considering depending on how much privacy you wish to maintain.

Once you have finished with your "Profile Setup," click "Save Changes." You can also look through some of the other options and choose any that interest you, but for the purpose of this exercise the next important tab is "Privacy."

If this were a personal YouTube account, I would potentially choose the reverse of these options, but you want maximum exposure for your Etsy shop and videos, so choosing the following configuration will allow as many people as possible to see your video:

▼ **Search and Contact Restrictions**

☐ Allow only friends to send messages or share videos

☑ Let others find my channel on YouTube if they have my email address

The above option means that as you share your e-mail address and make new contacts, they will be able to find your channel on YouTube.

Upload

When you're ready to upload your movie, simply click on the "Upload" option at the top of the page:

On the next page click on "Upload video," and you will need to browse to the location on your hard drive where you stored your Picasa video. Then click "Upload video." While you're waiting for your

video to upload, you could start to fill in the description for your video and tags. You can also include your Etsy shop's URL above your description.

This is how I would fill out the options:

> **Title:** Sea Glass Jewelry Designs on Etsy (*note my keyword is used at the front of the title*)
>
> **Description:**
>
> http://www.etsy.com/yourestyshop
>
> Sea Glass Jewelry created by (Your Etsy Shop Name). Here are some samples of my Sea Glass Jewelry designs and the photographs were taken on my local beach. I hope you enjoy my work and if you would like to see more then please visit my URL.
>
> **Tags:** "your etsy shop tags here"
>
> **Category:** Howto & Style
>
> **Privacy:** Public (anyone can search for and view—recommended

Music

If you want a soundtrack for your video, then there is an excellent free (and legal!) service called AudioSwap, which will allow you to use music with your images, and rather than your having to hunt for public domain music to use legally, it's all done for you.

To use AudioSwap, click on the drop-down

menu next to your video, then click on "Audio-Swap":

On the next page, you'll get a menu of different genres and artists, and clicking on each genre brings a host of choices. I find "Soundtrack" seems to work for these videos, as vocals can distract attention from the images, although this is a personal choice.

You can also see a thumbnail of your video and click "Preview" to see how your video will look using the selected music. Once you find the right track, simply click on "Publish."

It may take a little time for your video to become public, so you will need a little patience. Once your video and music have been rendered and uploaded to YouTube, you should be able to find your video by searching for the name of it within YouTube's search box.

Once you've found your video, you can promote it using Su.pr, Facebook, Twitter, et cetera, and you should also make a new blog post and embed your video and publish. The more places you show the video, the more visitors it will get.

It also helps if you can get some thumbs-up and positive reviews and comments, so the more people you e-mail the link to the better. Perhaps you could start a new post on Etsy's forum and ask people to leave constructive criticism and comments in exchange for a similar service.

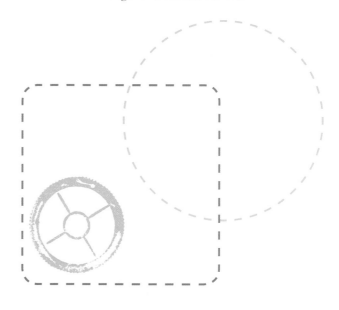

ACTION STEPS

- Download Picasa's free software.

- Deselect images that you do not wish Picasa to have access to.

- Create a folder for your best Etsy images and ensure this folder is in an easy-to-remember location on your hard drive.

- Create your first film with screen titles and a URL to your Etsy shop; preview the movie before saving it to your computer.

- Sign up for a YouTube account using your Etsy shop's Google account.

- Include your Etsy URL within your YouTube profile.

- Upload your movie and write a description, including relevant tags.

- Ensure your video is "public."

- Select a music track for your video, using AudioSwap.

- Promote your video using StumbleUpon, Twitter, and Facebook. Return to your We Love Etsy page, Squidoo, and HubPages and any other Web 2.0 sites that you have joined, ensuring you post your new video.

Conclusion

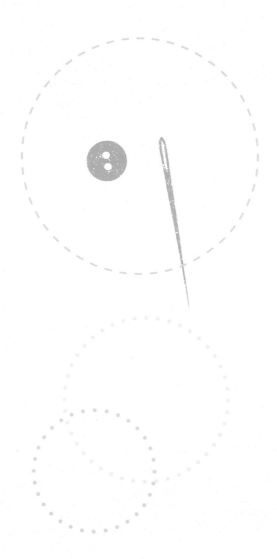

CONGRATULATIONS! You've reached the end of these tutorials. By completing each of the chapters and taking action you will have optimized your Etsy shop and begun to build a wide and varied presence both within Etsy and across the Internet.

If you found some of the lessons overwhelming, don't worry; simply go back and tackle one at a time. The wonderful thing about the Internet is that you can continually add more and more content and strengthen your brand and presence on a daily basis. The more work you put into building backlinks to your Web site (by adding new HubPages or Squidoo lenses or articles), the more likely your site will rank higher and the more you help people to find your work.

It's absolutely vital that you take every advantage to expand your presence online; by now I hope you can see the difference between selling a few items in a brick-and-mortar store and putting your creations before the world via the Internet.

Another great reason to set up a shop on Etsy is that you can fine-tune your store, constantly making changes and improvements as you find new techniques and tips.

As well as the suggestions contained within this book, you can find additional ideas for improving your shop by being active on the Etsy forums and Web sites such as We Love Etsy. The same goes for the other lessons in this book; the Web 2.0 sites I have included are always evolving and being updated. You can keep abreast of all the new changes by using Google Reader and by subscribing to the Web site's feeds, which helps you to stay one step ahead and with minimal effort. Simply set up a new Google alert or subscription to a Web site such as Etsy or Flickr, for example, and receive updates whenever new content or features are added.

Perhaps the most important exercise when it comes to selling online (or offline) is to be honest with yourself. Take time to look at your photography, adverts, and banner and your online presence—are you putting in 100 percent? If you know you have a weak area, then focus on improving it. If you're not sure, then ask others; there are plenty of critique postings in the Etsy forums.

You need to optimize your shop and present your creativity in the best possible light, and the time spent doing this is as important as the time spent creating. Even if you're selling online as more of a hobby than a business, you still want your art and creativity to reach the widest audience possible.

So congratulations once again! Not only have you invested your time and effort into completing this book and learned a brand-new way of building an online presence, but you've also created new art or crafts, jewelry or sock monkeys— something that wasn't there before!

Now it's time to give people the chance to recognize your creativity and genius!

Please stop by my Web site:

howtosellyourcraftsonline.com/

where you can browse the FAQs and find videos with additional information.

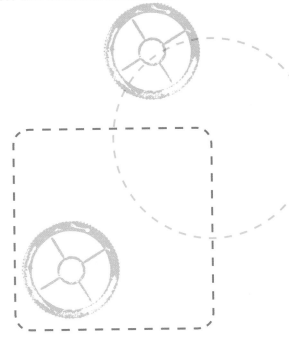

Online Resources

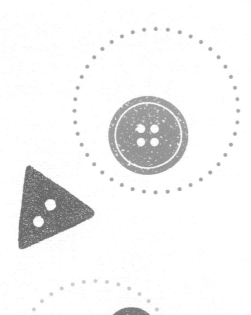

Selling Crafts

etsy.com

Additional Information To this Book

howtosellyourcraftsonline.com

Business Cards, Postcards, and Promotional Materials

us.moo.com

vistaprint.com

Packaging (and Tripods, Gadgets, and Other Things You May Need!):

ebay.com

packagingsupplies.com

Creating Graphics and Videos

fiverr.com

picasa.google.com

picnik.com

pixlr.com

youtube.com

Analyzing Your Shop's Traffic and Etsy Statistics

craftcount.com

craftcult.com/heartomatic.php

google.com/analytics

Internet Trends

google.com/insights/search

google.com/trends

Googlemail and Other Google Services

mail.google.com/mail/signup

google.com/local/add/businessCenter

google.com/voice

google.com/alerts

google.com/reader

Finding a Domain Name

instantdomainsearch.com/

Webhosting

hostgator.com

Blogging

blogger.com/home

livejournal.com

wordpress.com

wordpress.org

Building Your Web Presence

etsylove.ning.com

stumbleupon.com

su.pr

flickr.com

twitter.com

search.twitter.com

tweetdeck.com

facebook.com

facebook.com/pages

squidoo.com

hubpages.com

tumblr.com

weebly.com

https://posterous.com

myspace.com

answers.yahoo.com

deviantart.com

ezinearticles.com

craigslist.org

Index

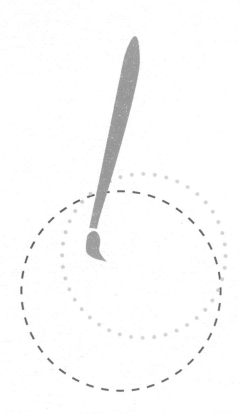

Notes